The MAILBOX®

The Education Center®

grades **PreK–K**

S0-AYS-111

Literacy for Little Learners

Fun-to-do activities that build key literacy skills!

- **Oral language**
- **Listening skills**
- **Phonological awareness**
- **Concepts of print**

- **Letter knowledge**
- **Letter-sound associations**
- **Letter formation and much, much more!**

Managing Editor: Gerri Primak

Editorial Team: Becky S. Andrews, Diane Badden, Kimberley Bruck, Karen A. Brudnak, Pam Crane, Lynette Dickerson, Tazmen Hansen, Marsha Heim, Lori Z. Henry, Debra Liverman, Dorothy C. McKinney, Thad H. McLaurin, Sharon Murphy, Jennifer Nunn, Mark Rainey, Laurel Robinson, Hope Rodgers, Donna K. Teal

www.themailbox.com

©2008 The Mailbox® Books
All rights reserved.
ISBN10 #1-56234-859-0 • ISBN13 #978-156234-859-5

Manufactured in the United States
10 9 8 7 6 5 4 3 2 1

Table of Contents

What's Inside 4

Alphabet Songs and Rhymes 5

A 6
B 9
C 12
D 15
E 18
F 21
G 24
H 27
I 30
J 33
K 36
L 39
M 42
N 45
O 48
P 51
Q 54
R 57

S 60
T 63
U 66
V 69
W 72
X 75
Y 77
Z 80
Multiple Letters 83

Letters and Sounds......163

Getting to Know Letters:
Centers 164

Getting to Know Letters:
Group Time 185

Beginning Sounds 193

Letter-Sound Associations 205

I'm going to tell you a T story.

A Print-Rich Classroom 89

Working With Names 90

Making Words Meaningful....... 111

Stories and Games...................131

Writing Words..........................149

Reproducible Picture Cards 220

What's Inside

135 print awareness activities

104 letter and sound activities

167 songs and rhymes

80 reproducible cards

Songs and Rhymes

Saying rhymes and singing songs nurtures listening skills and encourages creative uses of language. Songs stimulate the brain, engaging children in a unique way and helping them remember things that might otherwise easily slip from memory. Singing even helps develop important early literacy skills such as phonemic awareness.

About This Section

- **Alphabetically Arranged**

  Songs and rhymes are arranged in order alphabetically according to the letter emphasized.

- **Pick and Choose**

  You can pick and choose with confidence because all the songs are sung to familiar tunes and incorporate common themes.

- **Extras to Enhance Learning**

  To add an extra special touch, some verses are accompanied by suggestions for enhancing learning. Others come with tips for simply adding to the singing, rhyming, and letter-knowledge fun!

- **Extending the Learning**

  You will find many ways to adapt and use the songs and rhymes in this book. Consider extending learning experiences in the following ways:
  - making song charts
  - making individual books for children
  - making big books
  - having children act out the songs and rhymes

I Love A Words

Introduce your students to words that begin with short *A* using this short, familiar tune.

(sung to the tune of "Skip to My Lou")

I love *A* words; how about you?
I love *A* words, yes I do.
I love *A* words. Here are a few:
Apples, ants, and *alligators* too!

Repeat the song, substituting other short A *words.*

A Sounds

These kid-pleasing lyrics will draw students' attention to both the long and short *A* sounds. You can bet they'll be singing this tune long after your lesson ends!

(sung to the tune of "Jingle Bells")

A, A, A, A, A, A
*A*s are all around.
We would all like to know—
What is *A*'s short sound?

/ă/, /ă/, /ă/, /ă/, /ă/, /ă/
/ă/ is what we say.
Do you know any words
That start the short *A* way?

Children's chant:
Apple, ant, and *alligator* too
Start with short *A*, yes, they do!

Repeat the song, substituting different short A *words in the chant. Or use the next verse to practice long* A.

A, A, A, A, A, A
*A*s are all around.
We would all like to know—
What is *A*'s long sound?

/ā/, /ā/, /ā/, /ā/, /ā/, /ā/
/ā/ is what we say.
Do you know any words
That start the long *A* way?

Children's chant:
Ape, acorn, and *April* too
Start with long *A*, yes, they do!

When You See an A

Gather picture cards for this fun tune and incorporate them into the song. Then keep them handy for a post-singing short A picture review.

(sung to the tune of "If You're Happy and You Know It")

When you see an *A* thing, shout, "Hooray!"
When you see an *A* thing, shout, "Hooray!"
Look for apples and astronauts;
Spy some ants and alligators.
There are lots and lots of things that start with *A*.
Hooray!

Repeat the song, substituting different short A words as desired.

Astronaut Bear

When a few readings of this poem are complete, have each child draw a picture of a short *A* item that astronaut bear might see from the air. Combine them into a class book for a fun letter-sound review!

Astronaut, astronaut, astronaut bear,
Waving at planes up in the air.

Astronaut, astronaut, astronaut bear,
Spotting *A* things from up there.

Anchors, apples, and little ants too.
Down on earth, there are quite a few.

Let's Look for A Today

(sung to the tune of "The Farmer in the Dell")

Let's look for *A* today.
Let's look for *A* today.
Heigh-ho, away we go.
Let's look for *A* today.

Ant starts with *A*.
Apple starts with *A*.
Alligator and *applesauce*,
They both start with *A*.

We See A Things

Before beginning this simple song, place several short *A* items plus a few non-*A* items in the center of your circle-time area. Then seat your students around the objects. While singing the song, substitute four students' names in the last four lines and have each child locate and pick up a short *A* item. Action!

(sung to the tune of "Are You Sleeping?")

We see *A* things.
We see *A* things.
Yes, we do!
Yes, we do!
[Child's name], pick up one thing.
[Child's name], pick up one thing.
[Child's name] too!
[Child's name] too!

I'm a Beautiful Bumblebee

After students are familiar with this rhyme, play this fun follow-up game. To prepare, draw or glue pictures of *B* and non-*B* words to paper flower cutouts. (If desired, use selected picture cards from pages 220–224.) Secure the flowers to the floor. Ask students to scurry around the room like bees while they recite the rhyme. When the rhyme ends, have each student stop on a flower only if it shows a *B* picture.

I'm a beautiful bumblebee.
I land on things that start with *B:*
Bunny and basket,
Butter and bread.
And when I'm tired,
I go to bed!

Let's Look for Bs Today

Students seek and find the letter *B* with this little ditty! After singing the song, have youngsters search the room for the letter *B*.

(sung to the tune of "The Farmer in the Dell")

Let's look for *B*s today.
Let's look for *B*s today.
Heigh-ho, just watch us go.
Let's look for *B*s today.

We found one on a block;
We found one in a book.
Heigh-ho, just watch us go.
We found some *B*s today.

The Bees on the Boat

Youngsters are all abuzz with this song and idea for the letter *B!* Write the song on a chart. Give each child a sticky note labeled with an uppercase or a lowercase *B*. As you sing the song, point to each child and have him place his sticky note over the corresponding letter on the chart. Buzzzz!

(sung to the tune of "The Wheels on the Bus")

Oh, the bees on the boat
Go buzz, buzz, buzz,
Buzz, buzz, buzz,
Buzz, buzz, buzz.
Oh, the bees on the boat
Go buzz, buzz, buzz.
Please let them off!

The bees on the boat,
They say, "Bye-bye,"
Say, "Bye-bye,"
Say, "Bye-bye."
The bees on the boat,
They say, "Bye-bye,"
And off they fly!

Bears Going to the Fair

Youngsters become dancing bear cubs when they act out this little ditty!

(sung to the tune of "Twinkle, Twinkle, Little Star")

Black bear, black bear
Brushes her hair.
She is going to the fair.
She will ride a bumper boat.
She will bob for apples that float.
She will buy two big balloons.
She will boogie to some tunes.

Pretend to brush hair.
Walk in place.
Pretend to steer boat.
Pretend to bob for apples.
Pretend to hold balloon strings.
Dance.

Brown bear, brown bear,
Brushes his hair.
He is going to the fair.
He will eat some berry pie.
He will bounce up in the sky.
He will smash some water balloons.
He will boogie to some tunes.

Pretend to brush hair.
Walk in place.
Pretend to eat pie.
Jump in place.
Pretend to toss water balloons.
Dance.

Baker Bear

There's a whole lot of letter tracing going on with this activity and rhyme. Write the rhyme on a chart. After reciting it, invite youngsters to use a blue highlighter to trace over each *B* on the chart.

Baker, baker,
Baker bear
Bakes berry pies
For the fair.

Blueberry, blackberry,
Boysenberry too.
I'll have blueberry!
How about you?

I Love B Words

(sung to the tune of "Skip to My Lou")

I love *B* words; how about you?
I love *B* words; yes, I do.
I love *B* words. Here's a few:
Baby, ball, and *bananas* too!

Repeat the song, substituting other B words.

My B Box

Students are eager to make a *B* box after reciting this rhyme. Simply label a large box with the letter *B* and have each child find a *B* item in the room and then place it in the box. Continue the collection, including items students bring from home if desired.

I have a big box.
I colored it blue.
I fill it with *B* things.
I have quite a few.

I have some boats
And some buttons and bows.
I have some balls
That I like to throw.

I take my box
Wherever I go.
I might need a *B* thing.
You just never know!

Three Baby Bunnies

After singing this song a few times, have students practice writing the letter *B* on their own funny money. Draw a simple dollar bill pattern with a *B* in the middle. Make copies so that each student has several. Let students trace the letter *B* onto each bill; then have them use the money for a dramatic presentation of this song.

(sung to the tune of "Three Blind Mice")

Three baby bunnies,
Three baby bunnies,
They're so funny
With their money.
They bought a baseball and a bat.
They bought a bow for a big blue hat.
They bought a beach ball but it went flat.
Three baby bunnies.

C

Clap for C

Gather an assortment of items whose names begin with the hard *C* sound and a few that don't begin with hard *C*. When youngsters have sung the song through, hold up an item and instruct them to clap if its name begins with hard *C*.

(sung to the tune of "Row, Row, Row Your Boat")

Clap, clap, clap your hands.
Clap your hands for *C*.
When you see a *C* thing,
Clap your hands for me.

/k/, /k/, /k/,
/k/, /k/, /k/

C Sounds

These kid-pleasing lyrics will draw students' attention to both the hard and soft *C* sounds. You can bet they'll be singing this tune long after your lesson ends!

(sung to the tune of "Jingle Bells")

C, C, C, C, C, C
*C*s are all around.
We would all like to know—
What is *C*'s hard sound?

/k/, /k/, /k/, /k/, /k/, /k/
/k/ is what we say.
Do you know any words
That start the hard *C* way?

Children's chant:
Cake, color, and *corn* too
Start with /k/; yes, they do!

Repeat the song, substituting different hard C *words in the chant. Or use the next verse to practice soft* C.

C, C, C, C, C, C
*C*s are all around.
We would all like to know—
What is *C*'s soft sound?

/s/, /s/, /s/, /s/, /s/, /s/
/s/ is what we say.
Do you know any words
That start the soft *C* way?

Children's chant:
Celery, cinnamon, and *circle* too
Start with /s/; yes, they do!

I Love C Foods

After singing this happy tune, have youngsters draw and label their favorite C foods on individual paper plates. Yum!

(sung to the tune of "Skip to My Lou")

I love carrots, yum, yum, yum.
I love cornbread, even crumbs.
I love candy; oh, what fun.
I love C foods in my tum!

I love corn, yum, yum, yum.
I love cookies, even crumbs.
I love cupcakes; oh, what fun.
I love C foods in my tum!

Cowboy Bear

Little cowpokes can eagerly help this cowboy bear by lassoing C words of their own. Program a supply of index cards with hard C words or pictures and some with non-C words or pictures. (If desired, use selected picture cards from pages 220–224.) Lay a length of yarn on the floor to resemble a lasso. Have each student draw a card, in turn, and then place only a C word card in the center of the lasso.

Cowboy, cowboy,
Cowboy bear
Rounds up C words everywhere.
Cows, cards, and *corn* too,
Cars and *coins,* to name a few.

I Love C Words

Grab a stuffed cat toy for this activity. After reciting the rhyme, show children the cat and then have them call out as many *C* words as they can for one to two minutes before the cat runs away (moves behind your back)!

"I love *C* words," said the cat.
"Like *cake* and *cookies*
And words like that."

How many *C* words can you say
Before the cat runs away?

clock

Let's Look for Cs Today

Students seek and find the letter *C* with this little ditty! After singing a couple of rounds of this song, have youngsters search the room for the letter *C*.

(sung to the tune of "The Farmer in the Dell")

Let's look for *C*s today.
Let's look for *C*s today.
Heigh-ho, away we go.
Let's look for *C*s today.

I Love D
(sung to the tune of "Skip to My Lou")

I love doughnuts and dump trucks too.
I love dinosaurs; how about you?
I love dessert when dinner is through.
I love *D*. Oh yes, I do!

D Sounds
(sung to the tune of "Jingle Bells")

D, D, D, D, D, D
Lots of *D*s around.
We would all like to know
How to make your sound.

/d/, /d/, /d/, /d/, /d/, /d/
/d/ is what you say.
We can say a lot of words
That start out this way.

*Encourage youngsters to suggest words
that begin with the letter* D *as you write
their suggestions on chart paper.*

Dunking Doughnuts!
You'll get requests by the dozens for this
sweet little song! Encourage youngsters to listen
carefully as they sing. Then invite them to identify words in the song that begin with *D*.

(sung to the tune of "Clementine")

Dunk your doughnut, dunk your doughnut
In the milk that's in your cup.
When it's gotten nice and soggy,
Then it's time to eat it up!

Down on the Farm

Welcome to the *D* farm! Repeat the song with your students, each time substituting a different word that begins with the letter *D* (see the suggestions below).

(sung to the tune of "Old MacDonald Had a Farm")

Dave and Dinah had a farm.
/d/, /d/, /d/, /d/, /d/
And on their farm they had some *D*s.
/d/, /d/, /d/, /d/, /d/
With a [dog] here and a [dog] there.
Here a [dog], there a [dog],
Everywhere a [dog], [dog].
Dave and Dinah had a farm.
/d/, /d/, /d/, /d/, /d/

Suggested words: duck, deer, donkey, desk, dish, door

What Could We See?

Little ones imagine things they could see that begin with the letter *D* when they perform this action rhyme!

D, D, what could we see?
What could we see that starts with *D?*
We could see daytime with the sun in the sky.
We could see ducks as they fly by.
We could see doughnuts so round and sweet.
We could see the dirt beneath our feet.

Point to eyes.
Throw hands outward with palms up.
Make a circle with arms above head.
Flap arms.
Rub tummy.
Stomp feet.

Down by the Duck Pond

Enrich a singing of this ducky little song by reviewing two *D* words found in the lyrics. Write the words *duck* and *ducklings* on chart paper. Invite children to point to the *D* in each word. Then explain that a duckling is a baby duck before diving into the song!

(sung to the tune of "Down by the Station")

Down by the duck pond,
Early in the morning,
See the little ducklings
Swimming in a row.
See the momma duck
So proud of all her ducklings.
Quack, quack, quack, quack.
Off they go!

Writing Letter *D*

Invite each youngster to write a *D* in the air with her index finger as she follows the steps given in this tune!

(sung to the tune of "The Muffin Man")

I love to write the letter *D,*
The letter *D,* the letter *D.*
First go down and then around.
It makes a *D,* you see!

Little Elf

Who better to introduce the sounds of letter *E* than a mischievous little elf? While students are away, stock your circle area with objects whose names begin with *E,* such as an envelope, egg, engine, elephant, and so forth. When students return, ask one student to pretend he's the little elf. Teach students the tune, and then lead them in singing the first verse. Have the little elf sing the second verse and name two of the objects.

(sung to the tune of "Are You Sleeping?")

What do you see
That starts with *E,*
Little elf,
Little elf?

I see an [name of object].
I see an [name of object].
You'll agree;
They start with *E.*

Repeat the song as desired, inviting a different child to name E *objects each time.*

E Sounds

This little ditty will engage your little ones while reinforcing short and long *E.* Excellent!

(sung to the tune of "Jingle Bells")

E, E, E, E, E, E
Lots of *E*s around.
Everyone would like to know—
What's your short *E* sound?

/ĕ/, /ĕ/, /ĕ/, /ĕ/, /ĕ/, /ĕ/
/ĕ/ is what we say.
Do you know of any words
That start the short *E* way?

Children's chant:
Eggs, elf, and *elephant* too
All start with short *e;* yes, they do!

Repeat the song, substituting different long E *words in the chant, or use the next verse to practice short* E.

E, E, E, E, E, E
Lots of *E*s around.
Everyone would like to know—
What's your long *E* sound?

/ē/, /ē/, /ē/, /ē/, /ē/, /ē/
/ē/ is what we say.
Do you know of any words
That start the long *E* way?

Children's chant:
Eagle, Easter, and *eel* too
All start with long *E;* yes, they do!

Engineer Bear

Here's an opportunity for extra practice with short *E*. Write this poem on chart paper, and then ask volunteers to wear an engineer's hat as they point to short *E* words.

Engineer, engineer,
Engineer bear,
Driving your train
From here to there.

Chugging past evergreens
And eggs in a nest.
Chugging past elk
All looking their best.

Chugging past elves
Out in the snow.
Chugging past elephants
In a circus show.

Elevator E

Elevator, elevator, elevator *E,*
Going up to floor number three.

Open the doors, and what do we see?
Only things that start with short *E!*

Engines with engineers, eggs of blue,
Elephants, eggplants, and envelopes too.

Elevator, elevator, elevator *E,*
Going up to floor number three.

Open the doors, and what do we see?
Only things that start with long *E!*

Eagles, eels, and Easter candy,
Easels and erasers—they come in handy!

Elevator, elevator, elevator *E,*
Going up to floor number three.

I Love E Things

Introduce your students to words that begin with long *E* using this short, familiar tune.

(sung to the tune of "Skip to My Lou")

I love *E* words; how about you?
I love *E* words; yes, I do.
I love *E* words. Here are a few:
Eagles, east, and *easels* too!

Repeat the song, substituting other long E *words.*

Let's Look for E Today
(sung to the tune of "The Farmer in the Dell")

Let's look for *E* today.
Let's look for *E* today.
Heigh-ho, away we go.
Let's look for *E* today.

Egg starts with *E.*
Engine starts with *E.*
Elephant and *evergreen,*
They both start with *E.*

Let's Fish for *F*s

Singing this *F* song is more fun when you play this simple magnetic fishing game too! On paper fish cutouts, write *F* words, such as *feather, fire, farm,* and *foot.* Then add a corresponding picture. Attach paper clips to the fish and string a magnet to a simple pole. Teach youngsters the first verse below. Then let your children take turns catching fish and reading the *F* words. When a child catches a fish, have her sing the second verse below, substituting her *F* word.

(sung to the tune of "The Farmer in the Dell")

Let's fish for *F*s today.
Let's fish for *F*s today.
Heigh-ho, away we go.
Let's fish for *F*s today.

I caught a [foot] today.
I caught a [foot] today.
Heigh-ho, just watch me go.
I caught a [foot] today.

Four Little Frogs

After your little ones enjoy singing a round of this song, ask volunteers to name other items that begin with *F.* Draw or write the name of each item on chart paper for all to see.

(sung to the tune of "Up on the Housetop")

Four little frogs went fishing one day.
One caught a feather, but it floated away.
One caught a football and threw it high.
One caught a fork just right for pie.

Fee, fie, foe! Watch them go.
Fee, fie, fum! Oh, what fun!
Four little frogs went fishing today.
What else did they catch? Can you say?

F

Swim Like Fish

Swim, hop, and toss—this movement song is sure to reinforce the *F* sound and get the wiggles out! Teach students the song while modeling fish movements. Then invite everyone to sing and move to the beat together. Ask students to listen for the word that begins with *F* in each phrase.

(sung to the tune of "Clementine")

[Swim like fish],
[Swim like fish],
[Swim like fish] just now.
Just now [swim like fish].
First, I will show you how.

Repeat the song, substituting a different movement verse each time, such as drift like feathers, toss a football, *or* fly like fairies.

Forest Bear

Encourage youngsters to listen for the *F* sound as you read this poem aloud. Ask each child to raise one finger each time he hears /f/. Then read the poem to your group, checking for understanding as you go.

Forest, forest,
Forest bear,
Greeting friends
Everywhere.

Four fast foxes,
Falcons that fly,
Five fine fish
Who passed right by.

Then one day
Bear heard a cry.
There was smoke
Up in the sky.

Bear rang the bell
To call the fire truck,
And soon the firefighters
Arrived; what luck!

They fought the fire
And put it out.
The forest animals
All gave a shout.

"Hip, hip, hooray
For forest bear
And brave firefighters
Everywhere!"

On a Farm

Farm begins with *F*. That's fantastic! Use this song with its simple repetition to help students focus on the word *farm* and its beginning sound /f/. Before singing, copy the song onto chart paper. Then invite volunteers to use a highlighter to circle the *F* words *farm* and *farmer.*

(sung to the tune of "London Bridge Is Falling Down")

Animals live on a farm, on a farm, on a farm.
Animals live on a farm with a farmer.

Cows and pigs live on a farm, on a farm, on a farm.
Cows and pigs live on a farm with a farmer.

Goats and sheep live on a farm, on a farm, on a farm.
Goats and sheep live on a farm with a farmer.

Hens and chicks live on a farm, on a farm, on a farm.
Hens and chicks live on a farm with a farmer.

Firefly, I See Your Light!

These fingertip fireflies will flit to *F* words in your classroom! Invite each child to press a fingertip onto a washable yellow stamp pad and then let his fingertip dry. Sing the song below with your youngsters and have each child use his yellow fingertip as a firefly while he explores the classroom, pointing to all the *F* words he can find. How enlightening!

(sung to the tune of "Shoo Fly")

Firefly, I see your light!
Firefly, I see your light!
Firefly, I see your light!
I see you shine on summer nights!

I'm a Little Gumball

When youngsters have sung this tune several times, invite them to practice writing the letter *G* on colorful gumball cutouts. Tape the gumballs to a large gumball machine cutout. Then display the gumball machine in the classroom. Sweet!

(sung to the tune of "I'm a Little Teapot")

I'm a little gumball
Round and small.
I don't cost very
Much at all.

You can put a penny
In the slot.
Turn the handle
And out I pop!

I Love *G!*

(sung to the tune of "Three Blind Mice")

I love *G.*
I love *G.*
Can't you see?
I love *G.*

I love gorillas at the zoo.
I also love grasshoppers; how about you?
I love to eat gallons of gumdrops too!
I love *G.*
I love *G.*

Writing the Letter *G*

While singing this kid-pleasing tune with your little ones, encourage them to use their index fingers to "write" the letter *G* in the air!

(sung to the tune of "The Muffin Man")

I love to write the letter *G,*
The letter *G,* the letter *G.*
I love to write the letter *G*
For everyone to see!

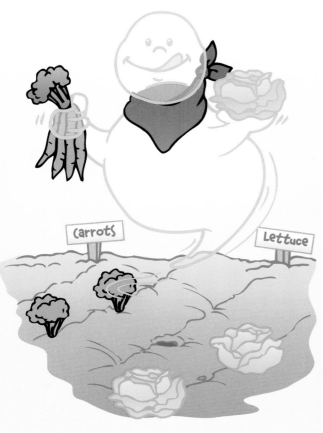

The Galloping Ghost

Introduce the words that begin with *G* in the lyrics below before your youngsters sing this "spook-tacular" song!

(sung to the tune of "My Bonnie Lies Over the Ocean")

The ghost gallops over the gate.
The ghost gallops over the tree.
The ghost gallops into the garden.
The ghost is hungry, you see!
Hungry, hungry, the ghost is hungry, you see, you see!
Hungry, hungry, the ghost is hungry, you see!

He gobbled up all of the garden,
Then giggled and twirled through the air.
Now we have to go to the grocery
And get all our vegetables there!
Hungry, hungry, the ghost was hungry, you see, you see!
Hungry, hungry, the ghost was hungry, you see!

Out in the Garden

Although gophers tend to be disliked by gardeners, they are perfect for studying the letter *G* in this song!

(sung to the tune of "Down by the Station")

Out in the garden,
Early in the morning,
See the little gopher
Digging all around.

He eats all the plants
And makes the gardener angry.
Then he hides in his tunnel
Under the ground.

Garbage Collection!

Display the words to this poem on sentence strips in a pocket chart. Then have youngsters locate words that begin with *G* before reciting the poem.

Garbage, garbage, garbage bear,
He gathers all the garbage everywhere!
His big truck rumbles as it goes down the road,
Stopping at each house to add to its load.

Where Is *G?*

Invite little ones to perform this song with easy-to-prepare puppets. Make an uppercase and a lowercase stick puppet similar to the ones shown for each child. Then have each student hold a puppet in each hand to perform the song!

(sung to the tune of "Where Is Thumbkin?")

Where is *G?* Where is *G?*   *Hold puppets behind back.*
Here it is! Here it is!   *Reveal one puppet, then the other.*
Can you say the *G* sound?   *Wiggle one puppet.*
Can you say the *G* sound?   *Wiggle the other puppet.*
/g/, /g/, /g/, /g/, /g/, /g/   *Wiggle both puppets.*

I Love *H*

(sung to the tune of "Three Blind Mice")

I love *H*.
I love *H*.
H is great.
H is great.

H is for *hot dogs* and *hamburgers* too.
H is hundreds of hugs for you!
H is a hat that is fancy and new.
I love *H*.
I love *H*.

Happy, Healthy, and Hungry!

Help your little ones learn the sound of letter *H* with an action song that focuses on descriptive words!

(sung to the tune of "Clementine")

H is happy;	*Point to smile.*
H is healthy.	*Hold up arms and show muscles.*
H is huge, and	*Stretch arms far apart.*
H is hot.	*Fan yourself.*
H is hungry;	*Rub stomach.*
H is handsome.	*Place hands on cheeks.*
H is helpful;	*Find a classmate.*
Thanks a lot!	*Shake the classmate's hand.*

The Hungry Horse

Review the sound of letter *H* with your students before singing this song. Once children have practiced the song several times, divide the students into two groups. Designate one group as horses and the other as farmers. Have the farmers perform the first stanza of the song, and the horses perform the final stanza!

(sung to the tune of "Are You Sleeping?")

Hungry horse,
Hungry horse,
Here's your hay.
Here's your hay.

Rub stomach.
Rub stomach.
Pretend to lay hay on the floor.
Pretend to lay hay on the floor.

Happy, happy horse,
Happy, happy horse,
Run and play.
Run and play.

Smile.
Smile.
Run in place.
Run in place.

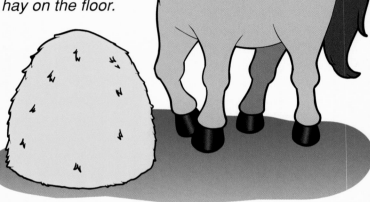

Hibernating Bear

Youngsters can "bear-ly" contain themselves when they listen to this silly poem! Encourage students to join in as you recite the poem several times. Then explain that everything the bear dreams of begins with the letter *H*. Invite students to suggest other things the bear could dream of that begin with *H*. Then encourage them to draw a picture of a dream for hibernating bear!

Hibernating bear doesn't make a peep.
What does he dream of in his sleep?
Does he dream of happy hikes on a hill?
Does he dream of honey pots he can fill?
Or how about a hippo in a party hat?
No, I'm sure he doesn't dream of that!

Up, Up, and Away!

Little ones' imaginations soar when they perform this cute song! Before the performance, be sure to have your students repeat the word *helicopter* several times and listen carefully to the sound of letter *H* at the beginning of the word.

(sung to the tune of "I'm a Little Teapot")

I'm a helicopter	*Point to self.*
On the ground.	*Point to ground.*
I flip my switch,	*Pretend to flip a switch.*
And my blades go around.	*Twirl around.*
When I get all revved up,	*Wiggle body.*
I can fly	*Point to self.*
Up, up, up	*Point up.*
Into the sky.	*Pretend to fly around the room.*

/h/

A Lovely Sound!

*(sung to the tune of
"She'll Be Comin' Round the Mountain")*

Oh, the letter *H* makes such a lovely sound!
Oh, the letter *H* makes such a lovely sound!
Well, I think we should all try it.
It says /h/. It's very quiet!
Oh, the letter *H* makes such a lovely sound! /h/, /h/

I'm a Little Inchworm

Make a path of picture cards in your classroom. Include pictures of items whose names begin with short *I* (such as *insect, infant,* and *instruments*) and others that don't. Teach your youngsters this silly song; then have them pretend to be inchworms inching past the pictures and nodding to those with names that begin with the short *I* sound.

(sung to the tune of "I'm a Little Teapot")

I'm a little inchworm,
Short and round.
I love to inch
Along the ground.

When I see something
That starts with short *I*,
I nod to it
As I inch by.

I Sounds

This little ditty will engage your little ones while reinforcing short and long *I*. Ideal!

(sung to the tune of "Jingle Bells")

I, I, I, I, I, I
Lots of *I*s around.
Everyone would like to know—
What's your short *I* sound?

/ĭ/, /ĭ/, /ĭ/, /ĭ/, /ĭ/, /ĭ/
/ĭ/ is what we say.
Do you know of any words
That start the short *I* way?

Children's chant:
Insects, inch, and *instrument* too
Start with short *I;* yes, they do!

Repeat the song, substituting different short I *words in the chant. Or use the next verse to practice long* I.

I, I, I, I, I, I
Lots of *I*s around.
Everyone would like to know—
What's your long *I* sound?

/ī/, /ī/, /ī/, /ī/, /ī/, /ī/
/ī/ is what we say.
Do you know of any words
That start the long *I* way?

Children's chant:
Icicle, idea, and *iron* too
Start with long *I;* yes, they do!

Inventor Bear

Inventing seems to come easy for this little bear!
After reading this poem with your little ones, see
what inventions they might be inspired to create.
Provide building blocks or other construction toys;
then give them time to bring their creations to life!
Encourage inventions that also begin with the letter
I. Inventor bear will be proud!

Inventor, inventor,
Inventor bear
Invents short *I* things
Everywhere.

Igloos so small
They fit only mice.
Itty-bitty instruments
The size of rice.

Instant tea
That glows when you drink.
Write in the air
With invisible ink!

Inventor bear
Is quite interesting.
I'd like to meet him
And see these things!

Imagine a Place

Inspire understanding of the short *I* sound
when you share this poem with youngsters.
After several readings, invite each child to raise
her pinky finger whenever she hears the short
I sound. Then have students brainstorm other
short *I* words to create additional verses.

Imagine a place where insects can talk.
Imagine a place where infants can walk.
Imagine a place where instruments play
All by themselves every day.
Imagine a world with interesting sights,
All of them *I* things. What a delight!

I Love *I* Words

Use this short, familiar tune to introduce your students to words that begin with long *I*.

(sung to the tune of "Skip to My Lou")

I love *I* words; how about you?
I love *I* words; yes, I do.
I love *I* words. Here are a few:
Icicle, iron, and *ivy* too!

Repeat the song, substituting other long I words.

Let's Look for *I* Today

(sung to the tune of "The Farmer in the Dell")

Let's look for *I* today.
Let's look for *I* today.
Heigh-ho, away we go.
Let's look for *I* today.

Ink starts with *I*.
Inside starts with *I*.
Invisible and *invitation,*
They both start with *I*.

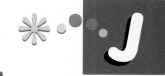

If You're Joyful

(sung to the tune of "If You're Happy and You Know It")

If you're joyful and you know it, [jump up high].
If you're joyful and you know it, [jump up high].
If you're joyful and you know it, then your actions surely show it.
If you're joyful and you know it, [jump up high].

Repeat the song, replacing the underlined phrase with dance a jig, *and* jog in place. *Then invite students to continue the song by creating other phrases featuring J words and actions.*

Judge Bear

Who knew there were so many *J*s to judge at the fair? Judge bear, of course!

Judge, judge,
Judge bear
Judged the contests
At the fair.

She judged the jams
And jellies too.
She sampled all;
There were quite a few.

She judged the riders
That jumped over things.
She judged the jeeps
That raced in a ring.

She judged the jitterbugs
That danced all day.
And she judged the jazz bands
That did swing and play.

She judged the jugglers
That juggled things high.
She judged the jets
That filled the sky.

Judge, judge,
Judge bear
Judged the contests
At the fair.

The Jet

Now boarding is this nonstop flight to *J* awareness! Before you sing with your youngsters, invite them to pretend their index fingers are jets and "fly" them each time they hear a *J* sound.

(sung to the tune of "My Bonnie Lies Over the Ocean")

The jet flew over the jungle.
The jet flew over the sea.
The jet flew over the mountain.
The jet flew over the tree.

Jet, jet, jet, jet
The jet flew over the sea-e-e.
Jet, jet, jet, jet
The jet just flew over me!

Jump for Jelly Beans

Sweeten *J* practice with this energetic letter-awareness song! Program a supply of large, colorful construction paper jelly beans with a variety of words that begin with *J* and some that begin with other letters. During a circle time, familiarize little ones with the song below, and then tell them that you want them to look for *J.* Sing the song together; then slowly cycle through the jelly bean words and have students jump for *J* words.

(sung to the tune of "Clementine")

Jump for jelly beans.
Jump for jelly beans.
Jump for jelly beans with *J.*
Just now jump for jelly beans.
Jump for jelly beans with *J.*

Jingle, Jingle

Invite a few children at a time to gently shake cluster bells or wrist bells as your whole class sings this song together. The perfect accompaniment to letter *J*!

(sung to the tune of "Are You Sleeping?")

Jingle, jingle. Jingle, jingle.
Jingle bells! Jingle bells!
I hear bells a-ringing,
Jing-a-ling-a-ling-ing.
Jingle bells! Jingle bells!

Jumping Jack

Encourage each youngster to pretend she is a jack-in-the-box while performing the words and movements in this fun action song.

(sung to the tune of "Are You Sleeping?")

Jumping Jack, Jumping Jack
Jumping up! Jumping back!
Hiding all the time
Until your box I wind.
Jumping Jack—out then back!

Jump from side to side with each beat.
Jump up high; then jump and crouch low.
Stay in a crouched position.
Pretend to wind an imaginary handle.
Jump up high; then jump and crouch low.

Let's Look for Ks Today

(sung to the tune of "The Farmer in the Dell")

Let's look for Ks today.
Let's look for Ks today.
Heigh-ho, away we go.
Let's look for Ks today.

Key starts with *K*.
Kitten starts with *K*.
Keyboard and *kindergarten*,
They all start with *K*.

K Sounds

This little ditty will engage your little ones while reinforcing the sound letter *K* makes.

(sung to the tune of "Jingle Bells")

K, K, K, K, K, K
Lots of *K*s around.
Everyone would like to know—
Just what is your sound?

/k/, /k/, /k/, /k/, /k/, /k/
/k/ is what we say.
Do you know any words
That start with letter *K*?

Children's chant:
Kite, kiss, and *kangaroo*
All start with *K;* yes, they do!

Repeat the song, substituting different K words in the chant.

Kick Your Feet

This active song is perfect to reinforce the /k/ sound while rousing your little sleepyheads after rest time. Be sure that each child has plenty of personal space and is lying on her back before beginning. Then invite children to gently kick their feet as described in the lyrics.

(sung to the tune of "Row, Row, Row Your Boat")

Kick, kick, kick your feet.
Kick your feet for *K.*
Kick them high.
Kick them low.
Kick them different ways.

Karate Bear

Karate, karate,
Karate bear
Has a blue belt
That he can wear.

He kicks for things
That start with *K,*
To protect *K* things
Day after day.

He kicks for kettles.
He kicks for keys.
He kicks for kites
Flying in the breeze.

He kicks for kitchens
And even kings.
He kicks for ketchup
Of all things.

Karate, karate,
Karate bear
Kicks for *K*s
To show he cares.

If You're Kind and You Know It

(sung to the tune of "If You're Happy and You Know It")

If you're kind and you know it, blow a kiss.
If you're kind and you know it, blow a kiss.
If you're kind and you know it, then your face will surely show it.
If you're kind and you know it, blow a kiss.

Continue with other verses that feature K such as "fly a kite" or "give a kick."

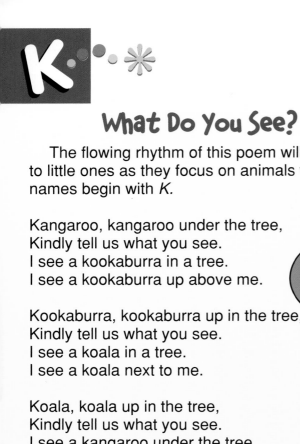

What Do You See?

The flowing rhythm of this poem will appeal to little ones as they focus on animals whose names begin with *K*.

Kangaroo, kangaroo under the tree,
Kindly tell us what you see.
I see a kookaburra in a tree.
I see a kookaburra up above me.

Kookaburra, kookaburra up in the tree,
Kindly tell us what you see.
I see a koala in a tree.
I see a koala next to me.

Koala, koala up in the tree,
Kindly tell us what you see.
I see a kangaroo under the tree.
I see a kangaroo under me.

"K-A-N-G-A!"

(sung to the tune of "Bingo")

This energetic little kangaroo will help raise *K* awareness while getting rid of the wiggles!

Verse: There is a kangaroo that [hops], and Kanga is her name-o.
Chorus: K-A-N-G-A, K-A-N-G-A, K-A-N-G-A, and Kanga is her name-o.

Repeat the song, substituting the underlined verb with knits, kicks, skips, *and so forth. Invite each child to perform the desired action as you sing the verse and chorus together.*

38

The Ls Are Leaping

Invite youngsters to perform some of the action words as they recite these lyrics, which accentuate *L* words!

(sung to the tune of "The Ants Go Marching")

Little [leaves] are leaping all around,
Some high, some low.
Large [leaves] are leaping all around,
Some high, some low.
Some go up, and some come down,
Spinning and swirling all over town.
Fluttering softly,
[Leaves] are leaping all around!

Repeat the song, replacing the underlined words with other L *words, such as* lizards, leprechauns, *and* lions.

I Love *L!*

(sung to the tune of "Three Blind Mice")

I love *L.*
I love *L.*
Yes, I do.
Yes, I do.

I love lions at the zoo.
I love lizards and llamas; do you?
I love licorice and lollipops too!
I love *L.*

Ladybug's Lunch

After your little ones have recited this poem, explain that ladybugs eat tiny bugs that live on leaves. Also have them listen for the /l/ sound at the beginning of *ladybug* and *leaf.* Give each child a leaf cutout and have her draw a few black dots for bugs, saying the /l/ sound as she draws each one. Finally, help each child glue a red pom-pom on her leaf for the ladybug. Munch, munch!

Once there was a ladybug,
Ladybug, ladybug.
Once there was a ladybug
Who landed on a leaf.

She stopped for a little lunch,
A little lunch, a little lunch.
She stopped for a little lunch.
Munch, munch, munch, munch, crunch!

Librarian Bear

Invite each youngster to make an L shape with his right hand, as shown, each time he hears a word that begins with the /l/ sound.

Librarian, librarian, librarian bear
Cares for books that she likes to share.

Books about lizards, lobsters, and bees.
Books about ladybugs landing on leaves.

Books about lazy lions and more.
Books about leopards and lambs galore!

Books about lemons, lettuce, and lunch.
Books about licorice and good things to munch.

Books about logs, lakes, and leaves.
Books about lands across the sea.

Librarian, librarian, librarian bear
Cares for books that she likes to share.

Lark's Song

Your little songbirds will enjoy performing the action described in the last line of each verse as you read this poem aloud. After reading the poem, ask each child to draw and color a picture of an animal whose name begins with the letter *L*. If desired, repeat the poem, replacing each animal and its action with youngsters' suggestions.

Larry the lizard
Listens to a lark.
Larry likes to hear its song
As he crawls in the dark.

Lucy the lion
Listens to a lark.
Lucy likes to hear its song
As she prowls in the dark.

Lenny the lobster
Listens to a lark.
Lenny likes to hear its song
As he swims in the dark.

Little Lizard

Your students will have lots of fun reciting this little rhyme and adding the fun actions. But don't limit your little ones! Ask them for more *L* word suggestions; then keep the verses coming!

Little lizard,
Little lizard,
What do you see?
I see a lobster
Looking at me.

Little lizard,
Little lizard,
What do you see?
I see a lion
Looking at me.

Little lizard,
Little lizard,
What do you see?
I see a ladybug
looking at me.

M

The Man in the Moon

After a few rousing rounds of this song to gain familiarity, separate students into two groups. Have the groups face each other, and then ask Group 1 to sing and act out the first verse, followed by Group 2 singing the second verse.

(sung to the tune of "The Muffin Man")

Have you seen the man in the moon,
The man in the moon, the man in the moon?
Have you seen the man in the moon?
He's watching over you.

Yes, I've seen the man in the moon,
The man in the moon, the man in the moon.
Yes, I've seen the man in the moon.
He can see you too!

The Mailman March

Invite your little tikes to march in place as you recite this song that celebrates the letter *M!*

(sung to the tune of "My Bonnie Lies Over the Ocean")

The mailman marched over a [marble].
The mailman marched over a [mop].
The mailman marched over the [marigolds],
To put my mail in the mailbox!

Mailman, mailman, delivering mail all day.
Mailman, mailman, lets nothing get in his way.

Repeat the song, replacing the underlined words with other M *words, such as* meadow, mountain, *or* moon.

The Moose Went Over the Molehill

Before reciting this fun song with youngsters, ask them to name *M* words. Record students' ideas on a chart to refer to later.

(sung to the tune of "The Bear Went Over the Mountain")

The moose went over the molehill.
The moose went over the molehill.
The moose went over the molehill.
What do you think she saw?

She saw a [mountain of money].
She saw a [mountain of money].
She saw a [mountain of money].
That is what she saw.

Repeat the song, replacing the underlined phrase with other M *phrases, such as* mound of mud, man in the moon, *or* messy mop.

Mama Mouse

As you read this poem to your little ones, ask them to show the sign language gesture for *M* each time they hear a word that begins with the letter *M.*

Mama mouse,
Mama mouse
Mixes mini muffins.

Mama mouse,
Mama mouse
makes milk shakes.

Mama mouse,
Mama mouse,
Where are the shakes and muffins?

Mama mouse,
Mama mouse—
She eats what she makes!

Motorcycle Bear

Your little cubs will memorize the /m/ sound after repeating this poem several times! After reading, ask each child to draw a picture of motorcycle bear doing an *M* activity. If desired, create a class book by stacking the pictures with a cover and stapling them together. It makes for mighty fine reading!

Motorcycle bear, motorcycle bear,
Motoring around without a care.

Motoring in the morning and midafternoon,
Making noise—vroom, vroom, vroom!

Motoring by [mountains], [meadows], and [moons].
Going and going, he really zooms!

Motorcycle bear, motorcycle bear,
Motoring around without a care.

Repeat the poem, replacing the underlined words with other M *words, such as* mailboxes, monkeys, *and* moose.

The *M* Café

After reading this poem, give each child a paper plate. Invite the child to draw her favorite food that begins with *M.* Then display the plates on an *M* display board covered in a plastic tablecloth.

Molly went to the *M* café,
And here's what the menu did say:

Muffins, marshmallows,
And macaroni too;
Milk shakes, melons,
And meatball stew.

Molly ordered a meal
Of meatball stew.
Then she munched some macaroni
And had a milk shake too!

Molly went to the *M* café.
I think she really enjoyed her stay.

Found a Necklace

After students become familiar with this song, invite them to take turns making up new verses with more *N* words.

(sung to the tune of "Clementine")

Found a new nest, found a new nest,
Found a new nest on the ground.
I put it back up in the tree,
Till the owner came around.

Found a necklace, found a necklace,
Found a necklace on the ground.
I gave it to a little girl
Who was looking all around.

Found a nut, found a nut,
Found a nut in a sack.
I gave it to a nutcracker
Who opened it with a crack!

Found a nose, found a nose,
Found a nose upside down.
I gave it to a silly man
Who was dressed up like a clown.

Nurse Bear

As you read this nurturing poem to youngsters, ask them to nod their heads each time they hear a word that begins with *N*.

Nurse, nurse,
Nurse bear,
Nursing others
With lots of care.

Changing nightgowns,
Putting on new sheets.
Wiping noses
And propping up feet.

Serving noodles,
Never making noise.
Reading nursery rhymes
To sleepy girls and boys.

Passing out nuts
For a nighttime treat.
Checking on little nappers
As they sleep.

Nurse, nurse,
Nurse bear,
Nursing others
With lots of care.

I Love *N* Words

Before sharing this nifty song, ask students to name words that begin with *N*. Record youngsters' answers on a chart and then refer to the words as you repeat the song.

(sung to the tune of "Skip to My Lou")

I love *N* words; how about you?
I love *N* words; yes, I do.
I love *N* words. Here are a few:
Name, nine, and *neighbor* too!

Repeat the song, substituting other N *words, such as* note, nod, *and* nature.

name   nod
newt   note
noodle   nine
number

I Looked in the Newspaper

After sharing the poem with your little detectives, give pairs of students a portion of a newspaper page (enlarge a copy if desired) and ask them to circle all the *N*s they spy.

I looked in the newspaper.
What did I spy?
Nine nifty *N* things
That I want to buy.

A nightgown, a nutcracker,
A necktie that's new.
A net and a nail
And a necklace for you.

A napkin, a nectarine,
A newt with spots!
Now it's off to the store
To buy lots and lots!

Let's Look for *N*s Today

In advance, prepare several *N* picture cards for youngsters to hold up as the group recites the song. (If desired, use selected cards from pages 220–224.)

(sung to the tune of "The Farmer in the Dell")

Let's look for *N*s today.
Let's look for *N*s today.
Heigh-ho, away we go.
Let's look for *N*s today.

Nest starts with *N*.
Neck starts with *N*.
Noodle, nose, and *number* too.
They all start with *N*.

O

I Like to Row for Short O

(sung to the tune of "My Bonnie Lies Over the Ocean")

I like to row in the river.
I like to climb up a tree.
I like to drive on the highway
To see short *O* things all around me.
O, O, O, O
I see short *O* things around me.
O, O, O, O
I see short *O* things around me.

I see otters in the water.
I see ostriches waving at me.
I see olives in the branches.
I see short *O*s all around me.
O, O, O, O
I see short *O* things around me.
O, O, O, O
I see short *O* things around me.

Repeat the song, substituting different short O words, such as octopus *and* oxen.

O Sounds

Use all or part of this song to reinforce short *O* and long *O* sounds.

(sung to the tune of "Jingle Bells")

O, O, O, O, O, O
*O*s are all around.
We would all like to know—
What is *O*'s short sound?

/ŏ/, /ŏ/, /ŏ/, /ŏ/, /ŏ/, /ŏ/
/ŏ/ is what we say.
Do you know any words
That start the short *O* way?

Children chant:
Octopus, octagon, and *otter* too
Start with short *O;* yes, they do!

Repeat the song, substituting different short O words in the chant, or use the next verse to practice long O.

O, O, O, O, O, O
*O*s are all around.
We would all like to know—
What is *O*'s long sound?

/ō/, /ō/, /ō/, /ō/, /ō/, /ō/
/ō/ is what we say.
Do you know any words
That start the long *O* way?

Children chant:
Open, over, and *oatmeal* too
Start with long *O,* yes, they do!

Little Otter

This silly little nonsense poem will help your little ones focus on the short *O* sound. If desired, write the poem on a chart and have students circle or point to short *O* words.

I went walking down the street
When an otter I happened to meet.

He looked lost and all alone,
So I took that little otter home.

I gave him olives and an omelet too.
We watched a movie about an ostrich in a zoo.

I guess he'd had enough to eat
Because he ran right out on his little otter feet.

Then the little otter ran back to his home.
Now I'm the one feeling all alone!

Opposites All Around

Fit in this fun song during your short *O* study, and your youngsters will not only help you point out that *opposite* begins with short *O*, but also get a lesson in opposites!

(sung to the tune of "Twinkle, Twinkle, Little Star")

Opposites, opposites, all around.
When I have a smile, you have a frown.
When I go fast, you go slow.
When I say, "Stop," you say, "Go."
Opposites, opposites, all around.
When I stand up, you sit down.

I Love O Words

(sung to the tune of "Skip to My Lou")

I love *O* words; how about you?
I love *O* words; yes, I do.
I love *O* words. Here are a few:
Ocean, open, and *overalls* too!

Repeat the song, substituting other long O
words, such as Ohio, oar, *and* old.

Let's Look for O Today

(sung to the tune of "The Farmer in the Dell")

Let's look for *O* today.
Let's look for *O* today.
Heigh-ho, away we go.
Let's look for *O* today.

Oval starts with *O.*
Oatmeal starts with *O.*
Oak and *oat* and *overcoat*—
They all start with *O.*

If desired, change this song to feature short
O *words. For added fun, bring in the* O
objects you plan to mention in the song,
so students can point to each one when
it's mentioned.

Pound Play Dough

Sing this playful song with a small group of youngsters. Then invite them to act out each verse. Give each child a small ball of play dough and encourage her to perform the actions as you sing the song together. After you sing the song, help students recognize that each object they formed begins with the letter P. What other objects beginning with P can they make with play dough?

(sung to the tune of "Row, Row, Row Your Boat")

Pound, pound, pound your play dough.
Pound it as flat as can be.
Plop it on a plate. Oh!
A pancake now you see.

Roll, roll, roll your play dough.
Roll it like a snake.
Pinch a point into one end.
A pencil you did make!

Shape, shape, shape your play dough.
Shape it like a ball.
Add a stem; then look again—
A pumpkin for the fall!

Pancake Man

Sing the song with youngsters several times, each time substituting a different P ingredient for the underlined words. Then give each child a construction paper pancake and have her draw her favorite perfect pancake ingredient!

(sung to the tune of "The Muffin Man")

Oh, do you know the pancake man,
The pancake man, the pancake man?
Oh, do you know the pancake man
Who makes [pickle] pancakes?

Oh, yes, we know the pancake man,
The pancake man, the pancake man.
Oh, yes, we know the pancake man
He makes [pickle] pancakes!

Penny Purchase

In advance, have each child find and cut out a magazine picture that begins with the /p/ sound. Then ask your students to sit in a circle holding their pictures. Recite the poem several times; each time ask two volunteers to show and name their *P* pictures in place of the underlined words.

I have a penny. What can I buy?
A picture, a pickle, or a pizza pie.

I have a penny. What can I get?
Some popcorn, a pillow, or a new pink pet.

I have a penny. What will I do?
Purchase some [plums] and a [puzzle] for you.

Pilot Bear

What does pilot bear see from way up in the air? Little ones are glad to offer their suggestions, which will come in handy as you expand on this simple rhyme. In advance, copy the poem onto chart paper. Write students' suggestions of *P* words on individual sticky notes. As you reread the poem, place students' words over the underlined words in the poem.

Pilot bear, pilot bear
Flying high up in the air.

Flying over [parks] and [porches].
Flying all around.
Flying over [pools] and [pastures].
What else has he found?

Pretty Package

Before reading this poem, fill a box with one or more items that begin with *P*. Then wrap the box as if it arrived in the mail addressed to your class. To build excitement, bring out the package just before reading the poem. Then share the poem and have students guess the contents of the package before having them unwrap it and reveal the surprise.

A pretty package at my door.
A pretty package from a store.

Is it a present, just for me?
I think I'll peek, so I can see.

I tear off the paper and peek inside.
It's a pink piggy bank—what a surprise!

Let's Look for *P*s Today

(sung to the tune of "The Farmer in the Dell")

Here's a simple song that's perfect for building vocabulary! Ask youngsters to list words that begin with *P* and record their answers on a chart. Repeat the song, substituting students' words for the underlined words.

Let's look for *P*s today.
Let's look for *P*s today.
Heigh-ho, away we go.
Let's look for *P*s today.

Puppy starts with *P*.
Pig starts with *P*.
[*Potato*] and [*pumpkin*],
They both start with *P*.

P

peas

popcorn

pizza

pig

potato

pear

I Like Q

(sung to the tune of "Three Blind Mice")

I like *Q*.
I like *Q*.
Yes, I do.
I like *Q*.

Q is for *quick* and *Q* is for *queen*.
Q is for *quilt* that is the color green.
Q is for *quarterback* on a team.
I like *Q*.
Yes, I do!

Asking Questions

Little ones have all the answers when you assist them in reciting this chant! If desired, make a set of cards with the following pictures: a quarterback, a queen, a quail, and a duck quacking. After reciting each question, hold up the appropriate card and help students identify the picture. When children become proficient at this activity, invite a child to choose and hold the picture cards!

Question, question number one:
Who throws footballs in the sun?
A quarterback!

Question, question number two:
Who has a crown with jewels of blue?
A queen!

Question, question number three:
Whose nest is not in a tree?
A quail!

Question, question number four:
What does a duck say when it wants more?
"Quack!"

A queen!

A Song About Q

Celebrate the letter *Q* with this catchy sing-along! Before introducing the song to your youngsters, explain that the word *recite* means to say something out loud.

(sung to the tune of "If You're Happy and You Know It")

Here's a little song about the letter *Q*.
There are words that start with *Q;* I'll list a few.
Quarter, quilt, quack, and *quite.*
There are more we could recite.
Here's a little song about the letter *Q.*

Queen Bear

The result of this royal poem and activity is a class full of smiling students! Write each line of the poem on a sentence strip, leaving a blank space each time the letter *Q* is used. Display the strips in order in a pocket chart. Then read the poem to your youngsters without the *Q*s. When the giggling subsides, explain to the students that the *Q*s are missing and need to be written in. Encourage children to observe closely as you write the missing letters. Finally, recite the corrected poem with your class!

Queen bear sits on her throne,
Counting her quarters all alone
Under a quilt made with golden thread,
With a queenly crown upon her head.

Four Quiet Queens

Spotlight the letter *Q* with this quirky chant about four quiet queens!

Four quiet queens sit all day,
Trying to think of something to say.
They quietly quilt till it's time to quit
Then they quickly eat a banana split!

Q and U

Use this poem to introduce youngsters to the partnership between the letters *Q* and *U.*

Q and *U* like each other a lot.
You'll find them together more often than not.
Quarter and *quiet*, *quilt* and *queen*
Are some of the words in which they're seen!

Red Robin

This rhyme is perfect for some springtime practice of the /r/ sound. Wrap up a reading of this rhyme with an outdoor walk to search for more *R* things.

Red robin, red robin
Up in the tree,
Name some *R* things
That you see.

I see rivers,
Rocks, and rainbows.
I see roosters
That like to crow.

I see raccoons,
Rabbits, and rats.
I see roses
And red rubber mats.

Red robin, red robin
Up in the tree,
Thank you for naming
Some *R* things for me.

Rancher Randy

Gather some bandanas or cowboy hats for your little ones when you introduce this song! Then send them galloping around the classroom on their pretend horses as they sing out a rousing round of this tune. Don't forget to rope in a beginning /r/ sound reminder as you introduce the song. Ride on!

(sung to the tune of "Yankee Doodle")

Rancher Randy came to town
For the rodeo.
He could ride, and he could rope.
He put on quite a show.

Round and round the ring he went.
Round and round he'd go.
He wore a hat and boots and chaps,
Dressed right from head to toe!

Noisy Robot

This little robot has quite a time staying upright when he bumps into many things, causing him to call out, "/r/!" Things aren't so good for the silly robot, but it is a great chance to remind your youngsters about the beginning sound /r/.

A rattling red robot
With round button eyes
Would often fall down
And then let out a cry!

Each time he bumped something,
He fell down.
"/r/," said the robot
As he landed on the ground!

"/r/," said the robot
as he bumped into a rock.
"/r/," said the robot
as he bumped into the clock.

"/r/," said the robot
as he bumped into the rack.
"/r/" said the robot,
"Help! I landed on my back."

From Rubbish to Recycled

I looked through the rubbish,
And what can I say.
Lots of *R* things were thrown away.

Ribbons and ropes and radios,
Roller blades with crunched-up toes.
Raincoats, rattles, and rickrack galore.
Rakes and rowboats without oars.

It seems like a shame
To just toss them away.
Maybe we could recycle today!

Rooster, Rooster, Running Around

Your little ones will have a rousing good time flapping their wings as they recite this *R* rhyme. Begin by asking students to list things that begin with the /r/ sound and recording their answers on a chart. Then repeat the rhyme several times, replacing the underlined words with words from the list.

Rooster, rooster, running around,
Looking for *R* things on the ground!
He found a [rock] and a [rabbit] that's blue;
He found a [ring] and a [radio] too!
Rooster, rooster, running around,
Looking for *R* things on the ground!

Riddle Rhymes

Your students just might want to create *R* riddles of their own after solving this first round!

Here are some riddles that also rhyme.
Can you guess each answer in record time?

In case you have trouble, here's a hint:
The answers are *R* words; that should help a bit.

The first one you tie, or you coil it round.
It's helpful to keep a tent tied to the ground.   *(rope)*

The next is real fast as it soars through space.
Astronauts might be found in this place.   *(rocket)*

This last one is wet when it falls from the sky.
You'll need an umbrella to keep you dry.   *(rain)*

S

I'm a Little Sailboat

(sung to the tune of "I'm a Little Teapot")

I'm a little sailboat,
Short and stout.
I have a sail
That moves about.

When I go out sailing,
I soak in the sun,
Seeking the sea
And its salty fun!

Sing a Song of Six Seals

(sung to the tune of "Sing a Song of Sixpence")

Sing a song of six seals
Sitting on the sand.
67 seagulls
Coming in to land.

When the seals look up
Into the sky,
The 67 seagulls
Just pass right by.

Sailor Bear

Ahoy there! Sailor bear is ready to sail into *S* practice!

Sailor, sailor, sailor bear,
Sailing his ship everywhere.

Sailing by seashells
On soft white sand.
Sailing by seagulls
And a lemonade stand.

Sailing by surfers
Out in the sun.
Sailing by seals
Having fun.

Sailing by sharks
And seaweed galore.
Sailing by sunbathers
Sitting on the shore.

Sailor, sailor, sailor bear
Sailing his ship everywhere.

Surfing

Surf's up! Encourage youngsters to pretend to paddle their surfboards out into the surf to catch a wave of *S* practice. Then invite children to sing together as they surf to shore. Hang ten!

(sung to the tune of "My Bonnie Lies Over the Ocean")

The surfer is out in the surf.
The surfer is out in the sea.
The surfer is out on his surfboard.
The surfer is little old me.
Surfing, surfing,
Surfing out on the sea, the sea.
Surfing, surfing,
The surfer is little old me!

A Sunflower Grows

Plant some *S* awareness when you recite this energetic poem with your little ones. Invite each child to perform the actions as you say the poem together. Then read the poem again with extra emphasis on the words that begin with *S*.

A sunflower starts with a tiny seed.	*Crouch down small like a seed.*
Soil, sun, and water	
Are what it needs.	*Pretend to pat soil around feet.*
A sunflower sprouts	
From something small	*Kneel with arms out.*
To something strong	
And straight and tall.	*Stand tall, arms out.*

The Sandwich Song

Sing a silly sandwich song to reinforce *S* awareness whenever there's a spare second before snacktime! Sounds scrumptious!

(sung to the tune of "I'm a Little Teapot")

I'm a little sandwich on your plate.
I have something special, just you wait.
Is it [salami]? Is it ham?
Can you guess just what I am?

Repeat the song, substituting the underlined word with different S words—the sillier, the better!

Ten Little Toes

Program a sticky dot with the letter *T* for each child. Have each youngster remove her shoes and socks and then place a programmed sticky dot on her index finger. As the song is sung, have each child use her finger to point to and count her toes.

(sung to the tune of "Ten Little Indians")

One little, two little, three little toes,
Four little, five little, six little toes,
Seven little, eight little, nine little toes,
Ten toes on my feet.

Teddy Bear

Recite this rhyme once and your cubs will be ready to act it out the second time through!

Teddy, teddy, teddy bear,
He likes to exercise anywhere.

He likes to tap all of his toes.   *Tap toes.*
He likes to touch the tip of his nose. *Touch nose.*
He likes to turn himself around.   *Turn around.*
He likes to tumble to the ground.   *Drop down to the floor.*

He likes to tiptoe way up high.   *Tiptoe.*
He like to toss things to the sky.   *Pretend to toss a ball in the air.*
He likes to tunnel under a chair.   *Pretend to crawl under a chair.*
He likes to exercise anywhere!

She'll Be Towing With Her Tugboat

Grab your toy tugboats (or blocks for pretend tugboats) and have youngsters use them to practice forming the letter *T* on the floor after singing this little ditty!

(sung to the tune of "She'll Be Coming Round the Mountain")

She'll be [towing with her tugboat] when she comes.
She'll be [towing with her tugboat] when she comes.
She'll be [towing with her tugboat],
She'll be [towing with her tugboat],
She'll be [towing with her tugboat] when she comes.

Repeat the song, substituting turning in her taxi *in each line of the song.*

Tiger Song

Little ones will have a growlin' good time singing this tune! As you sing the song in the same manner as "Bingo," have children say the /t/ sound instead of clapping as a substitute for each of the letters.

(sung to the tune of "Bingo")

Deep in the jungle lives a cat,
And Tiger is his name-o.
T-I-G-E-R, T-I-G-E-R, T-I-G-E-R,
And Tiger is his name-o.

/t/, /t/, /t/

Ticktock

Get ready to hear the /t/ sound 60 times over! After singing this song, have each child watch the second hand on a large clock and say the /t/ sound with each tick of the hand.

(sung to the tune of "Are You Sleeping?")

"Tick, tick, tock,
Tick, tick, tock,"
Says the clock,
Says the clock.
/t/, /t/, /t/, /t/, /t/, /t/
/t/, /t/, /t/, /t/, /t/, /t/
Tick, tick, tock,
Tick, tick, tock.

Teacher Bear

There's a whole lot of teaching going on after reading this rhyme. Invite each youngster to "teach" the class how to write the letter *T,* describing the strokes as he writes.

Teacher, teacher,
Teacher bear,
Teaching students
About the sun, moon, and air.

Teaching about numbers
And our ABCs.
Teaching about fun stuff,
Like writing *T*s.

Teacher, teacher,
Teacher bear,
Teaching students
Everywhere!

U Sounds

These kid-pleasing lyrics will draw students' attention to both the long and short *U* sounds.

(sung to the tune of "Jingle Bells")

U, U, U, U, U, U
*U*s are all around.
We would all like to know—
What is *U*'s short sound?

/ŭ/, /ŭ/, /ŭ/, /ŭ/, /ŭ/, /ŭ/
/ŭ/ is what we say.
Do you know any words
That start the short *U* way?

Children's chant:
Under, up, and *uncle* too
Start with short *U;* yes, they do!

Repeat the song, substituting different short U words in the chant, or use the next verse to practice long U.

U, U, U, U, U, U
*U*s are all around.
We would all like to know—
What is *U*'s long sound?

/ū/, /ū/, /ū/, /ū/, /ū/, /ū/
/ū/ is what we say.
Do you know any words
That start the long *U* way?

Children's chant:
Use, unit, and *ukelele* too
Start with long *U;* yes, they do!

Umbrella Song

Sit under an open an umbrella while you share this cheery tune with youngsters. Then turn over the umbrella and pass around a bowl filled with a class supply of die-cut alphabet letters (be sure to include plenty of *U*s). Invite each child to take a letter and name it. If it's a *U,* encourage her to place it in the umbrella. If it's another letter, have her place it in her lap. Continue in this manner until each child has had a turn and the bowl is empty.

(sung to the tune of "I'm a Little Teapot")

Here's my new umbrella,
Wide and high.
It keeps me cozy, warm, and dry.
If the rain starts falling from the sky,
Just open it up, and you'll stay dry!

My Uncle

Short *U* is Uncle Upton's favorite sound!
When students are familiar with this poem,
invite them to make the sign for *U,* as
shown, each time they hear the short *U*
sound.

Uncle Upton walked under a bridge.
Uncle Upton sat under a tree.
Uncle Upton carried an umbrella
And kept all the rain off me!

The Unicorn

Share this poem with students; then invite
each child to pretend she is a unicorn by putting
her index finger on her head to resemble a
horn. Then have her use her horn to point out
examples of *U* in your classroom. How useful!

There once was a horse
Who was old and gray.
He wanted to look different
Somehow, someway.

He wished he were white
And knew how to fly.
He got his wish,
And he took to the sky.

His coat is now white.
On his head is a horn.
He has two wings.
He's a unicorn!

under

I Love *U* Words

Introduce your students to words that begin with short *U* using this short, familiar tune.

(sung to the tune of "Skip to My Lou")

I love *U* words; how about you?
I love *U* words; yes, I do.
I love *U* words. Here are a few:
Up, umpire, and *umbrella* too!

Repeat the song, substituting other short U *words.*

Let's Look for *U* Today

(sung to the tune of "The Farmer in the Dell")

Let's look for *U* today.
Let's look for *U* today.
Heigh-ho, away we go.
Let's look for *U* today.

Unload starts with *U.*
Upstairs starts with *U.*
Umbrella and *underwear,*
They both start with *U.*

My Valentine

As you sing this song to youngsters, ask them to give a thumbs-up each time they hear a *V* word.

(sung to the tune of "Three Blind Mice")

Valentine, valentine,
Please be mine; please be mine.
I'll play the violin for you.
I'll bring violets, oh so blue.
I'll wear a vest if you promise to
Be my valentine!

The Letter V

Encourage each child to write the letter *V* in the air with her index finger as you share this poem.

Can you make the letter *V?*
It's as easy as can be.
Slant line down,
Slant line up.
Very good *V!*

My Very *V* Vacation

Gather some *V* picture cards to incorporate with this song. Have youngsters sit in a circle and sing the song. Then show them two picture cards at a time to replace the underlined words as you repeat the song.

(sung to the tune of "My Bonnie Lies Over the Ocean")

Last summer we went on vacation.
My dad drove our van down the road.
We traveled down to a valley,
Then to a volcano we rode.
V, V, V, V
Vacationing is for me, for me.
V, V, V, V
There is so much to see.

The van drove past some villages.
We stopped at a very nice town.
I bought some [vases] and [violins],
And a violet velvet gown.
V, V, V, V
Vacationing is for me, for me.
V, V, V, V
There is so much to see.

I Love V Words

(sung to the tune of "Skip to My Lou")

I love *V* words; how about you?
I love *V* words; yes, I do.
I love *V* words. Here are a few:
Violin, video, and *vegetables* too!

Village Adventure

Capture students' attention with this very *V*-filled verse!

Once in a village, on a dark, dark night,
I spied a very funny sight:

A vampire with a violet bat,
A vulture and a velvet cat,

Some volleyballs on twisty vines,
And a van full of valentines.

In this place with its silly scene,
Would you believe it was Halloween?

Wish and Wink

Wishing and winking entice youngsters to stay on task as they learn the /w/ sound! Encourage students to wink each time they hear the /w/ sound as you sing the song. Then ask youngsters to list other *W* words and write them on a wish word wall. Repeat the song, replacing each underlined word with a word from the word wall.

(sung to the tune of "My Bonnie Lies Over the Ocean")

I wish I had three wishes.
I know just what I would do.
If I had three wishes,
I'd wish for *W*s!

Wink, wink, wink, wink,
I'd wish for [watches], [wagons], and [worms].
Wink, wink, wink, wink,
They all begin with *W*!

walrus
watercolor
woodchuck
wave
weeds

Window Watch

Encourage youngsters to perform the action words as you recite this poem.

I washed the window and what did I see?
A wide-eyed walrus staring at me.

I watched him waddle and wiggle.
I watched him wash in the waves.
I watched him dive in the water,
And then I watched him wander away.

Wave for the Waiter

Your little waiters and waitresses will enjoy the wild *W* menu in this poem. In advance, create several word picture cards with *W* words such as *watermelon, weeds, worm, water, watch,* and *wagon.* Read the poem aloud to students. Then show them two picture cards and repeat the poem, replacing the underlined words each time. Just for fun, have two students at a time act out the poem.

I wave for the waiter.
I don't like to wait.
I am very, very hungry
And there's nothing on my plate.
"What do you wish?"
Asked the waiter at last.
"I'll have [waffles] with [walnuts],
And please make it fast!"

I'll Be Riding on a Wave

Encourage youngsters to name *W* words to replace the underlined word, such as *windmill, walrus, washing machine,* and *wooden boat.*

(sung to the tune of "She'll Be Comin' Round the Mountain")

I'll be riding on a [wave],
When I come.
I'll be riding on a [wave],
When I come.
I'll be riding on a [wave].
I'll be riding on a [wave].
I'll be riding on a [wave].
When I come.

Wiggles

Get the wiggles out with this fun fingerplay. Encourage youngsters to move the corresponding body part(s) as they wiggle their way to quiet time.

I wiggle my fingers;
I wiggle my toes.
I wiggle my shoulders;
I wiggle my nose.
Now no more wiggles are left in me,
So I'm as still as I can be.

Little Wiggle Worm

Your little wiggle worms will be ready to learn after several renditions of this active poem.

(sung to the tune of "I'm a Little Teapot")

I'm a little wiggle worm;	*Wiggle body.*
Watch me go!	
I can wiggle fast	*Wiggle fast.*
Or very, very slow.	*Wiggle slow.*
I wiggle all around,	*Wiggle and turn around.*
Then back I go,	
Down to the ground	*Wiggle and bend down low.*
To the home I know.	

X-Ray Bear

Gather all your little doctors and show them a real X ray to introduce this extra special rhyme.

X-ray bear,
X-ray bear,
She looks at X rays
For breaks and tears.

She takes a picture
Of your body inside.
She takes a picture
Where nothing can hide.

She looks at your bones.
Does she see a break?
She knows from the X rays
What treatment to make.

Xs and Os

Chances are some of your youngsters already know about *X*s and *O*s, so let them reveal the special symbols of love to the class. As you recite the poem, ask a small group of students to use their bodies to form an X shape. Then give each child a sheet of construction paper to create a special XOXO card for a loved one.

A card came in the mail today.
It's filled with *X*s and *O*s.
I wish I knew just what they mean.
Does anybody know?

X means kisses.
O means hugs.
When you get them,
The card's filled with love.

X Marks the Spot

X marks the spot for exercise fun! In advance, make a class set of X puppets similar to the one shown. Then have each child use a puppet to gently tap the appropriate body part as you recite the poem.

X marks the spot,
Head, shoulder, toes.

X marks the spot,
Tummy, knee, nose.

X marks the spot,
Foot, heel, elbows.

X marks the spot—
Now everyone knows!

Ox With a Box

Introduce youngsters to words that *end* with X with this excellent poem! To prepare, write the poem on a chart. Read the poem as you point to each word. Then give a child a highlighter to mark each word that ends with X. Put the chart at a center for students to read and write the -*x* words.

This is the ox
Who has a box.
An ox with a box is he.
Inside the box he has a fox,
A fox for all to see!

Yarn for Sale

Bring out some balls of yarn in a variety of colors to help this poem come to life. Use colored tape to mark a *Y* on each one. After students are familiar with the poem, encourage some volunteers to each hold a ball of yarn. Read the poem again. When a word is read that begins with *Y,* have them hold the balls of yarn high and then lower them again.

Yarn for sale, yarn for sale,
Yellow, red, green, and blue.
Yarn for sale, yarn for sale,
Some for me and some for you.

Enough to make a sweater
Or a scarf in blue and green.
Or maybe yellow slippers,
Nicest that I've ever seen.

Yo-Yo Bear

Give your students a demonstration of a yo-yo in action. Small as it is, it's difficult to keep it moving all the time. After an intentionally fumbled demonstration, read the poem aloud and then point out how talented yo-yo bear is to be able to yo-yo *anywhere.* Finally, mention how talented your students are at finding the /y/ sound in words they hear. Can they find some *Y*s in this poem? You bet!

Yo-yo bear, yo-yo bear,
He can yo-yo anywhere!
On a couch or on a chair,
Over here or over there!
Yo-yo bear, yo-yo bear,
He can yo-yo anywhere!

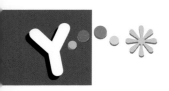

yawn!

Involve your students in singing this animated song and you know they'll pick up on the /y/ sounds as they yawn their way to the end of the tune.

(sung to the tune of "My Bonnie Lies Over the Ocean")

At night when it's dark and I'm sleepy,
When my bedtime story is read,
I yawn 'cause I'm feeling so tired,
Which means it's time to go to bed.
Yawn, yawn, it's time for me to go to bed, to bed!
Yawn, yawn, it's time for me to go to bed!

Raise arms as if yawning.
Raise arms as if yawning.

The Letter Y

(sung to the tune of "There's a Hole in the Bucket")

There's a letter named *Y*,
Named *Y*, named *Y*.
There's a letter named *Y*,
Oh, where is it found?

Well, it's found in *yard*.
And *yogurt* and *yawn*.
And it's found in *yellow*,
And /y/ is its sound!

Yummy Food

Put this song on the menu for some /y/ sound recognition! After a hearty helping of singing practice, lead your little ones in a discussion about their favorite foods.

(sung to the tune of "If You're Happy and You Know It")

Can you name a yummy food you like to eat? (Yum! Yum!)
One you like so much that it's your favorite treat? (Yum! Yum!)
It's a food that tastes so good;
You'd eat it always if you could.
Can you name a yummy food you like to eat? (Yum! Yum!)

The Sound of Y

Your youngsters can't wait to help fill this song with their own *Y* word choices. Substitute their selections for the underlined words as you sing the song again and again.

(sung to the tune of "The Farmer in the Dell")

The letter *Y* says /y/.
The letter *Y* says /y/.
In *[yak]* and *[you]* and *[yellow]* too,
The letter *Y* says /y/.

Zip and Zoom

Practice the letter *Z* and introduce youngsters to different types of transportation with this zooming little song. In advance, collect several different toy vehicles, such as cars, boats, planes, rockets, and trains. Each time you repeat the song, show youngsters a different vehicle to replace the underlined word.

(sung to the tune of "Zip-a-dee-doo-dah")

Zip-a-dee-doo-dah, zip-a-dee-ay,
I like to zoom-zoom around all day!
I am a(n) [race car] zooming this way.
Zip-a-dee-doo-dah, zip-a-dee-ay!

ZZZZZOOOOOMMMMM....

Zookeeper Bear

Have your little zookeepers think of different animals to feed each time you repeat this rhyme.

Zookeeper bear,
Zookeeper bear,
Helping animals,
Zany and rare.

He feeds the animals
At the zoo.
He feeds the [zebras]
And [kangaroos].

Zookeeper bear,
Zookeeper bear,
Helping animals,
Zany and rare.

Animals Live in the Zoo

Your little learners will be full of zeal as they think of different animals to add to this fun song. For added impact, make a "zoo" flash card to show every time the word is read.

(sung to the tune of "Mary Had a Little Lamb")

Animals live in the zoo,
In the zoo, in the zoo.
Animals live in the zoo.
Let's go there and see some!
[Zebras] live in the zoo,
In the zoo, in the zoo.
[Zebras] live in the zoo.
Let's go there and see some!

A Zippy Tune

Zip right into practicing the /z/ sound by inviting each child to use his jacket or bookbag to zip up! Have youngsters sit in a circle wearing or holding their zippered items. Invite them to zip their zippers as you sing the song. Repeat the song several times, replacing the underlined word with another zippered item.

(sung to the tune of "If You're Happy and You Know It")

If your [coat] has a zipper, zip it up!
If your [coat] has a zipper, zip it up!
If your [coat] has a zipper,
Bet you're feeling pretty chipper!
If your [coat] has a zipper, zip it up!

Counting Zebras

Your little herd of zebras will enjoy zigzagging around as you sing this fun counting song. Have youngsters sit in a circle and then select one child to be the zebra. Lead your group in chanting the first verse of the rhyme as the zebra gallops around the outside of the circle. Then have the zebra choose another child from the herd to join him. Chant the verse again, this time saying *two, zebras,* and *they* in place of the underlined words. Continue in this manner until your whole herd is galloping about! Then chant the final verse and have your herd act out the movements.

(chanted to the rhythm of "One Elephant Went Out to Play")

[One] little [zebra] went out to play
On the savanna one fine day.
[He] had such enormous fun
[He] asked another zebra to come!

The zebra herd went out to play
On the savanna one fine day.
They grew tired as they ran around,
So they all lay down!

I'm a Hungry Little Frog

Fibbit, gibbit, hibbit—this kid-pleasing chant encourages silly consonant sound substitution! After chanting the verse below, substitute a different consonant sound in each repetition. If desired, end each round of substitutions with *R* so the hungry little frog can spend the rest of his day ribbiting!

I'm a hungry little frog
Swimming all around.
I just ate a [B],
So I'm making silly sounds.

When I have something
Important to say,
I open my mouth
and [bibbit] all day!

[Bibbit, bibbit, bibbit.
Bibbit, bibbit, bibbit].
I open my mouth
and [bibbit] all day!

Bibbit!

Letter Baby Rap

This rap is terrific for reinforcing consonant-sound awareness. Each time you repeat the rap with students, substitute a different consonant sound.

[B] baby, [B] baby,
What do you say?
"[/b/] baby. [/b/] baby,"
That's what I say.

[S] baby, [S] baby,
What do you say?
"[/s/] baby, [/s/] baby,"
That's what I say.

Mud Pie

This round-robin chant provides letter and name reinforcement for everyone in your class! Teach little ones the verse below. Then insert a child's first initial and name into the rhyme where appropriate. Invite the named child to repeat the rhyme, saying a classmate's initial and name. Continue chanting until each child has had a turn to include a classmate's name in the verse.

Mud pie, mud pie in your hand.
Think of a name as fast as you can.
Roll it, pat it, and mark it with a(n) [D].
Then bake it in the sun for [Danny] and me!

The Loading Up Song

Ahoy! It's time to load up with letter-sound awareness. Sing the first verse with youngsters; then slowly add a verse each time you discuss a different letter's sound. If desired, include props and encourage students to act out each verse.

(sung to the tune of "Row, Row, Row Your Boat")

Fill, fill, fill your boat.
Fill your boat with [A]s—
[Ants], [apples], and [alligators];
Then sail across the sea.

We Love Letters

Here's a ditty designed to reinforce any letter you wish! Simply substitute the desired letter and words where appropriate.

(sung to the tune of "Skip to My Lou")

Let's sing about the letter [T].
Let's sing about [T] words we see.
[Tires], [toast], and [target] too.
Oh, letter [T], you're loved by me.

Someone in Our Class

Bet your students' names begin with lots of different letters! Use this song to reinforce letter-sound awareness while giving each student a moment in the spotlight.

(sung to the tune of "I've Been Working on the Railroad"—the third verse: "Someone's in the kitchen with Dinah…")

Someone in our class is named [Kelli].
Someone in our class, we know.
Someone in our class is named [Kelli].
And [she] would like to say hello!

What Do I See?

Spotlight beginning sounds in words with this adaptable call-and-response chant! Make several picture cards for a chosen letter. (If desired, use selected picture cards from pages 220–224.) After reviewing the letter's sound, hold up a picture card and have students name the picture. Then lead students in the chant below. Continue by introducing other picture cards and repeating the chant, substituting other letter and picture names as appropriate.

Teacher: *[B]*, *[B]*; what do you see?
What do you see that begins with *[B]*?
Children: I see a [bear]; that's what I see,
That's what I see that begins with *[B]*!

Jingle Jangle

This silly song is so much fun to sing, your little ones won't realize they are learning to substitute letter sounds! If desired, give each child a jingle bell bracelet or tambourine for added musical enjoyment. Then lead children in singing the song four times, substituting a different set of words from the suggestions provided each time.

(sung to the tune of "Twinkle, Twinkle, Little Star")

Jingle, jangle, jingle, jangle.
Everybody, jingle, jangle.
It's a very happy sound.
Jingle, jangle all around!
Jingle, jangle, jingle, jangle.
Everybody, jingle, jangle.

Suggested words: *bingle, bangle; tingle, tangle; pingle, pangle*

A, B, C, D, Sing With Me

Once your little ones are familiar with this chant, encourage them to make up additional verses to continue through the alphabet.

A, B, C, D, sing with me;
These are letters that I see.
A is for *apple.*
B is for *ball.*
C is for *cat.*
D is for *doll.*
A, B, C, D, E, F, G,
These are letters that I see.
E is for *eggs.*
F is for *fish.*
G is for *goat.*
Don't you wish
That we could sing the whole day through
About the letters from A to *Zoo!*

The Alphabet Poem

This alphabet poem will help youngsters make valuable letter-sound connections.

A is for *airplane.* B is for *buck.*
C is for *cookie.* D is for *duck.*
E is for *elephant.* F is for *fog.*
G is for *gate.* H is for *hog.*
I is for *igloo.* J is for *jam.*
K is for *king.* L is for *lamb.*
M is for *monkey.* N is for *nail.*
O is for *octopus.* P is for *pail.*
Q is for *queen.* R is for *rose.*
S is for *soap.* T is for *toes.*
U is for *umbrella.* V is for *vase.*
W is for wind blowing in my face.
X is for *X ray.* Y is for *you.*
Z is for *zebra* in the *zoo.*

The Alphabet Letters Bake

Use this poem before snack time to stir up a batch of alphabet sequencing! On a table, display in random order 26 frosted cupcakes, each decorated with a different alphabet letter. Gather little ones at the edge of the table. As you read the poem aloud, point to the corresponding cupcakes. During a second reading, assist the students in arranging the cupcakes in alphabetical order. Next, lead the students in naming the letters in sequence. Then invite each child to select a cupcake for snack. Store the remaining cupcakes or send them home with little ones at the end of the day.

A asked for it.
B baked it.
C cut it.
D decorated it.
E enjoyed it.
F finished it.
G gobbled it.
H hid it.
I iced it.
J jiggled it.
K kept it.
L loved it.
M made it.
N nibbled it.
O observed it.
P poked it.
Q quartered it.
R reviewed it.
S smelled it.
T tasted it.
U, V, W, X, Y, and *Z* cleaned the kitchen.

A Print-Rich Classroom

An early childhood classroom filled with print offers children countless opportunities to learn about letters and sounds, to develop word awareness, and to learn the concepts of print.

- Part of creating a print-rich classroom involves displaying lots of labels, signs, and other kinds of print, such as charts or displays featuring children's thoughts, preferences, or recollections.

- Other crucial aspects are providing a developmentally appropriate classroom library and reading books aloud—especially big books—so that young children are exposed to concepts of print in the meaningful context of stories.

- No aspect of a print-rich classroom is more influential than the conversation that surrounds the use of print. It's the talk about print that can help children see different aspects of letters or words they haven't yet noticed. By directing children's attention to things such as where to begin reading or similarities and differences in words, we foster their understanding of how print works.

Working With Names

This section consists of ideas to help students:

- encounter their names in print

- use their names to learn about how letters, sounds, and words work

- interact with their names and the names of their classmates

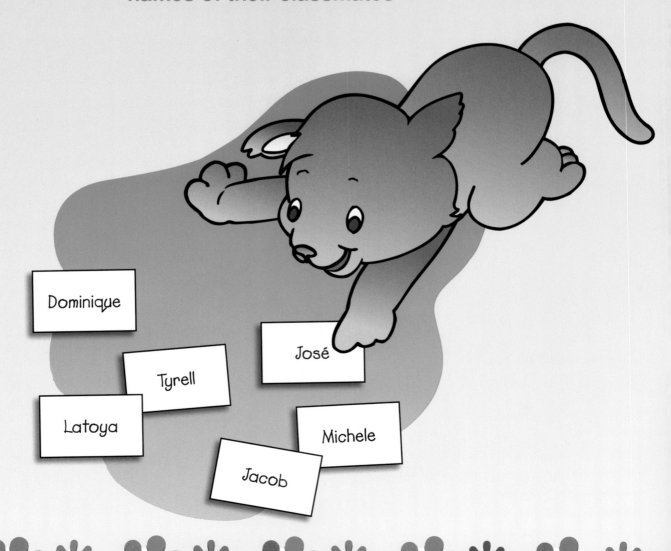

Name Pictures

These personalized pictures are child pleasing!

1. Write each child's name in pencil on an 8" x 11" piece of poster board.
2. Use a glitter glue pen to cover the pencil lines.
3. When the names are dry, have each child place a sheet of white paper on top of her glitter glue name and make a rubbing of her name with the side of a crayon.
4. Have her decorate her name rubbing with crayons, markers, or stickers.
5. If desired, place the glitter glue names at a center. Have youngsters use their fingers to trace the letters in each name.

Marvelous Magnets

These personalized magnets are a cinch to create, and they make perfect gifts.

1. For each child, cut a small rectangle from a Magnetic Canvas sheet. (A 9" x 12" sheet makes twelve 2¼" x 4" rectangles.)
2. Help each child use an oil-based paint marker to write his name on a rectangle.
3. Have him decorate his magnet with small stickers.
4. Use the magnets to display artwork on a magnetic board.

Name Bracelets

These name bracelets will keep students' names constantly in sight.

1. Cut paper or ribbon strips for bracelets.
2. Write each child's name on a strip with a marker or fabric pen.
3. Tape each child's bracelet around his wrist.
4. As conversation about letters occurs throughout the day, remind children to look for those letters on their name bracelets.

Nametags

As seasons and themes change throughout the year, use a touch of creativity to add interest and eye appeal to student nametags.

1. Cut geometric or seasonal shapes out of poster board, wallpaper, or other thick, textured paper.
2. Write each child's name on a shape.
3. Glue a clothespin on the back of each nametag.

Extension: Along with your other uses for nametags, use them with the game below.

Name-Matching Game

Here's a fine name-matching game children can play using the bracelets and nametags described above.

1. Place children's name bracelets in a bag.
2. Have them clip on their nametags and sit in a circle.
3. Have them take turns drawing a name bracelet out of the bag.
4. Each child looks at the name on the bracelet and matches it to the tag worn by the bracelet's owner.

Name Necklaces

Making and wearing these personalized necklaces will give your little ones extra reasons to focus in on the special features of their names.

1. Cut a 36-inch strip of crepe paper streamer for each child.
2. Label 1½-inch squares, one letter per square, to spell each child's name.
3. Provide each child with a crepe paper streamer, squares that spell his name, a nametag (or other spelling model), and a glue stick.
4. Assist him in arranging his squares to spell his name and gluing the squares to his streamer.
5. Tie each child's necklace around his neck.
6. Throughout the day, bring up letter-related topics and encourage youngsters to examine each other's necklaces in search of the letter being mentioned.

Name Frames

These frames are great for displaying children's work and their names.

1. Cut out a colored tagboard frame for each child (approximately 9" x 12" or 12" x 18").
2. Die-cut each child's name from a different color of tagboard.
3. Help each child glue her name along the bottom of the frame. Have her decorate the remainder of the frame using crayons or stickers.
4. Use the frames to display class work, artwork, or messages.

Name Stamps

Name stamps reinforce literacy skills, and they make nice gifts to children at the end of the year.

- Keep name stamps in your writing center for children to use when writing notes and cards to each other.
- Use name stamps to make a name lotto game.
- Use name stamps to stamp two index cards to make a set of each child's name, and place the cards at a center. Then ask each child to match pairs of name cards.

♥	Allison	Jake
Amy	Michael	Leanne
♥	Sue	Kevin

Letter Square Cutouts

Students will be proud of these name pictures.

1. Cut large letters from newspapers and magazines.
2. Place the appropriate letter cutouts for each child's name in an envelope along with his name card.
3. At a center, have each child glue his letter cutouts onto a piece of paper to spell his name. (Have him look at his name card if needed).
4. Have each child decorate his name paper with markers, stickers, or pictures cut from magazines.

Name Placemats

Here's an art project that is useful as a snacktime placemat.

1. Give each child an 18" x 24" piece of construction paper with her name written across the middle.
2. Set out markers, stickers, or crayons, and ask each child to decorate her name paper.
3. Laminate all the projects and use them as placemats.

Floor Mats

Have students make placemats especially for these floor activities.

- When you want children to have a partner for an activity, set the placemats on the floor in pairs and have each child find his placemat and his partner.
- Use the mats for your circle-time seating arrangement. Spread the mats on the floor in your circle-time area and then ask each child to find his mat.
- Place the mats on the floor to have children line up in a certain order.
- Take the mats outside for sitting on the grass.

Play Dough Names

Here's some name recognition practice your children can really sink their fingers into!

1. Prepare for each child a large laminated name card to use as a guide. (Or use the placemats described on page 95.)
2. Place play dough and the name cards at a center.
3. Show youngsters how to roll snakes and twist them into letters.
4. Have each child roll snakes and place them over each letter of her name card to create a play dough name.

Fingerpainted Football Jerseys

These child-made name jerseys are sure to score a touchdown with your little ones!

1. Cut a large football jersey shape from fingerpaint paper for each child. Then use masking tape to spell each child's name on a different jersey. Also, tape a number of the child's choice to the jersey as shown.
2. Have each child fingerpaint his cutout completely, covering the tape too.
3. When the paint is dry, carefully remove the tape.
4. Display the jerseys for all to enjoy.

Fabulous First Letter

Emphasize the beginning letter of each child's name with this sparkling activity.

1. Write each child's name on a sheet of tagboard, excluding the first letter.
2. Place alphabet sponges and a shallow pan of glue on a covered table.
3. Have each youngster in a small group find the beginning letter sponge for his name.
4. Help each child dip his sponge into the glue and then press it onto the appropriate space on his tagboard.
5. Help him sprinkle one of the the following items onto the glue print: sand tinted with powdered tempera paint, glitter, or confetti.

Variation: These can be made seasonal by adjusting the color of paper or art materials used or by cutting the paper into large seasonal shapes.

Dot-to-Dot Names

Keep a supply of these fun dot-to-dot sheets in your writing center for children to practice writing their names.

1. Make a dot-to-dot of each child's name, and then make several copies of each one.
2. For each child, affix a copy of his school photo to a folder and place the copies of his dot-to-dot name inside. Store the folders at your writing center.
3. Place markers or large crayons at the center for each child to use to connect the dots in his name.
4. Have him start at the top of each letter and follow the dots down, around, up, or across.

Class Greetings

Look for opportunities for your children to send fun cards on special occasions.

1. Set out a large piece of poster board (with an appropriate message) and markers.
2. Ask each child to write his name around the message.
3. Fold the poster board in half to form a card and have youngsters decorate the front.
4. Help students deliver the card or prepare it for mailing.

Teaching Sleeves

These slick sleeves can be used over and over for writing practice.

1. Purchase a class supply of plastic page protectors.
2. Write each child's name on a separate sheet of paper.
3. Place each sheet in a page protector.
4. Place the page protectors, crayons, dry-erase markers, and paper towels at a center.
5. Ask each youngster at the center to find her name sheet and then trace each letter.
6. Have students use paper towels to clean the protectors.

Magnetic Letter Match

Here is a clever use for alphabet magnets.
1. For each child, use alphabet magnets to trace the letters of his name onto a strip of tagboard.
2. Place magnets (enough for each child to spell his name) and name strips at a center.
3. Have each child find the matching magnetic letters and place them on top of the letters on his strip.

Writing Names

Create a special writing center with alphabet magnets.
1. Give each child a sheet of writing paper and a pencil.
2. At the top of his writing paper, set the magnetic letters that spell his name.
3. Have each child use the letters as a guide as he writes his name on the paper.

Class Voting

Need to gather some data for a class vote? Try using students' names.

1. Think of things that children can vote on, such as these:
   - What to have for snack: crackers and cheese or apple slices?
   - What decorations to go on the classroom door: ladybugs or frogs?
   - What gift to make for Mother's Day: a picture frame or a flowerpot?

2. Put a large sheet of chart paper on a wall at students' eye level. Make a T chart. Put pictures and words at the top of each column to indicate choices.

3. Set out markers or crayons and have children take turns writing their names in the column of their choice.

Mother's Day Gift

🌼 flowerpot	▭ picture frame
Shandi	Kinsey
Jesse	Mike
Ron	
Larry	
Sandy	

Beth   Lori

Friends Book

Your children will love reading this book, which features all their classmates, as they learn to recognize names.

1. Take pictures of each child doing an activity at school.

2. Prepare a class album with one or two pictures per page.

3. Write each child's name clearly on a strip of paper and glue it under the appropriate picture.

4. Set the album in your reading area for youngsters to enjoy.

5. Change the photos often to spark new interest in the book.

Name Card Search

Get the day off to a great start with a name-recognition task.

1. Make a name card for each child.
2. Place the cards around your room in prominent places.
3. Every morning, have each child search for his name card.
4. If a child has trouble finding his name, give him some clues.
5. Have youngsters return the cards to a predetermined spot, or have them keep the cards to use during morning activities.

Name Dismissal

Try using name cards for dismissing children from circle time or at the end of the day. One of the benefits of this activity is that children soon start recognizing each other's names as well as their own.

1. Hold up one or two name cards at a time.
2. When a child sees her name, she gets ready to go home or to the next activity.
3. At first, say each name as you hold up the cards, but gradually hold up the cards without any other prompting.

Letters in My Name Game

Here is a great circle-time game using letter cards for learning letters and names.

1. Give each child a personalized card.
2. Pick a letter to emphasize, and show its letter card.
3. Have each child look at her name card to check for the letter you are holding.
4. If she has a matching letter, have her raise her hand.
5. Have her hold up her name card for the others to see as she points to the correct letter.
6. When appropriate, say the child's name slowly, emphasizing the sound of each letter, especially the featured letter of the day.

Clothesline Names

This is a popular activity—indoors or outside.

1. Set up a clothesline between two chairs.
2. Draw uppercase letters on tagboard cards. Prepare letters as your class list requires.
3. Place the letters in a basket near the clothesline.
4. Set out plastic clothespins and prepare a card for each child with his name written in uppercase letters.
5. One at a time, have each child find his name card and choose the matching letters from the basket. Provide assistance as necessary.
6. Have him clip the letters on the line in the correct order to spell his name.
7. Have him remove the letters and place them back in the basket.

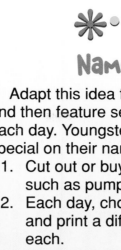

Name Puzzles

Adapt this idea for the current season, and then feature several different children each day. Youngsters will certainly feel special on their name days!

1. Cut out or buy colored seasonal shapes such as pumpkins, hearts, or apples.
2. Each day, choose two to four shapes and print a different child's name on each.
3. Cut each shape into two puzzle pieces.
4. Mix up the puzzle pieces and place them on a table.
5. Have youngsters take turns matching the name puzzles.
6. If desired, set out corresponding name cards for the children featured on the shape puzzles.

Fishing for Names

Over time, this game will enable children in your class to recognize each other's names.

1. Cut out and personalize one fish shape for each child in your class.
2. Attach a paper clip to each fish (be sure it doesn't cover up the name). Place the fish on blue paper shaped like a pond.
3. Make a fishing pole by tying a magnet to a string; then attach the other end of the string to a pole or wooden spoon.
4. Have youngsters take turns fishing for names.
5. Let each child catch three or four fish or as many as he can within a few minutes.
6. When a fish is caught, help the student read the name on the fish and then put it back in the pond.

Valentine Game

Use this fun game to celebrate learning names before, during, and after Valentine's Day.

1. Cut out a class set of five-inch heart shapes.
2. Write each child's name on a heart.
3. Place the hearts in a decorated box or basket.
4. Have children sit in a circle on the floor.
5. Choose a child to be the mail carrier and have her remove a heart from the basket.
6. Help her read the name on the heart and then deliver it to the correct child.
7. When the heart is delivered, have everyone say, "Hooray, hooray, hooray! [Riley] got a valentine today!"
8. Continue playing by having the valentine recipient become the next mail carrier.

Flannelboard Friends

Your kids will love matching their friends' faces with names in this game.

1. Copy pages 161 and 162 onto tagboard to make a class set of boy and girl patterns. Also gather a photo of each child and cut a two-inch circle from it.
2. Have each child color a pattern. Then use a permanent marker to write each child's name on the pattern. Laminate the patterns and cut them out.
3. Laminate the photos. Then place a small piece of Sticky-Tac adhesive on the back of each face.
4. Glue felt onto the back of each pattern.
5. Place several patterns on a flannelboard. Place the face circles in a box near the flannelboard.
6. Have children take turns pairing each face to the pattern with the matching name.
7. Put the patterns in the box and store it near the flannelboard for children to practice with during free time.

Name Stories

Here is a great language activity that also teaches children how to recognize each other's names.

1. Cut several small index cards in half.
2. Write each child's name on a card.
3. Place the cards in a bag or box.
4. Read a story to the class, stopping to draw a card and replace a character's name with the child's name.
5. Have youngsters take turns drawing a name out of the box and reading it, with your help, as you continue the story.

Spin a Name

Easy-to-make spinners are a fun way to substitute student names as you read a story to the class.

1. Take one or more paper plates and divide them into six to eight sections each.
2. Write a different child's name in each section.
3. Use a brad to attach a large paper clip to the middle of each plate for a spinner.
4. Read a story to the class, stopping to spin for a child's name to replace a character's name.
5. Let youngsters take turns spinning for a name and reading it, with your help, as you continue the story.

Cubby Tags

Youngsters will quickly learn to recognize their names when they look at their cubbies every day!

1. For each child, make a nametag sized to fit the cubbies in your classroom.
2. Place a seasonal or other special sticker on each nametag.
3. Laminate the nametags and attach each one to the appropriate cubby.

Attendance Chart

With this pocket attendance chart, your children can plunge into literacy as soon as they arrive each morning.

1. Buy or make a pocket chart with enough pockets for each child to have one.
2. Personalize each child's pocket with his name and photograph.
3. Make name cards and lay them on a table near the pocket chart.
4. When a youngster comes in each morning, he finds his name card and then inserts it into his name pocket.
5. Check the name cards remaining on the table to see who is absent.

Two Little Children

Two little children
Came to school:
One named [Jake],
And one named [Cole].
[Jake] said, "Hi."
[Cole] said it too.
They each made a friend
That day at school.

Name Rhymes

Here is a rhyme that incorporates children's names.

1. Have a child draw two name cards from a class set to use in the poem shown.
2. As you use a child's name in the verse, show the corresponding name card to the class.
3. Repeat the rhyme several times using different names.

Zoo Friends

As children's names are used in this poem about a trip to the zoo, youngsters may just squeal their agreement or denial.

1. Have a child draw four name cards from a class set to use in the poem below.
2. As you use a child's name in the verse, show the corresponding name card to the class.
3. Repeat the rhyme several times using different names.

The Zoo

[Mike] and [Eli] went to the zoo.
[Keesha] and [Lauren] went there too.
[Mike] liked the bears,
[Eli] liked the cockatoos,
[Keesha] liked the rattlesnakes,
And [Lauren] liked the kangaroos.

"Name-o"

Help students recognize and spell their names and those of their classmates with this adaptation of a traditional tune.

1. Write each letter of a child's name on a separate card.
2. Have students stand in front of the class and hold the cards to spell one child's name.
3. Sing the song, chanting the spelling of the child's name in the third line.
4. Sing about one child's name each day until every child has had a turn to hear her name.

(sung to the tune of "Bingo")

There is a friend who's in our class,
And [Abby] is her name-o!
[A-b-b-y], [A-b-b-y], [A-b-b-y],
And [Abby] is her name-o!

Clap Your Hands
(sung to the tune of "If You're Happy and You Know It")

If your name is [Hayley], clap your hands.
If your name is [Hayley], clap your hands.
If your name is [Hayley], clap your hands, and we'll clap too.
If your name is [Hayley], we'll clap for you!

Clap Your Hands

Your children will love the way even longer names fit easily into this song.

1. Have a child draw one name card from a class set to use in the song.
2. As you use a child's name in the song, show the corresponding name card to the class.
3. Repeat the song several times using different names.

Rainbow Letters

Use this colorful idea to help youngsters practice writing their names.

1. Use a yellow highlighter to print each child's name on several sheets of paper.
2. Give each child one sheet and have him trace the letters using three different colors of crayons.
3. Store the extra copies at a center for continued practice.

Golf Tee Names

Here's some name recognition and letter formation practice that will suit your children to a "tee"!

1. Label an eight-inch square of thick foam for each child as shown.
2. Place the squares, some golf tees, and a small rubber mallet in a center.
3. In turn, have each child hammer golf tees into the foam along the lines in his initial.
4. When he completes the activity, have him remove the tees from his square so they may be reused.

is for Jonathan

Name Sticks

Reinforce children's first and last names with these inexpensive name sticks.

1. Ask a local paint store to donate a class supply of paint-stirring sticks.
2. Draw a line down the center of each stick.
3. Have each child paint each half of her stick a different color.
4. Write each child's first name on the first half of her stick and her last name on the last portion of the stick.
5. Attach the hook sides of two self-adhesive Velcro fasteners to the back of each stick as shown.
6. Attach the corresponding loop sides of the Velcro fasteners to each child's desk or table.
7. Use the sticks for various name activities and to easily regroup students.

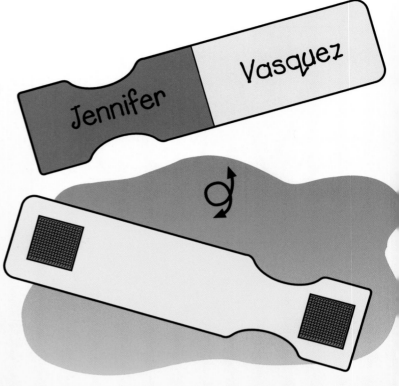

Name Chains

Here is a great way to help children learn the letters in their names.

1. Cut light-colored paper strips for making chains.
2. Write a letter on each strip so that you have appropriate uppercase and lowercase letter strips for each child to complete his name.
3. Have each child meet you at a work area and get the letter strips he will need to make a chain with his name on it.
4. Have each child lay out his letters on a table and place them in the proper order to spell his name.
5. Assist him in gluing the strips into a chain, starting with the first letter in his name.
6. Hang a string across two high points in your room and suspend each name chain from the string.
7. Have each child point out his name chain to others.

Making Words Meaningful

This section consists of:

- **ideas to make words meaningful to children**

- **ideas for labels, signs, charts, and more**

- **holiday and seasonal ideas**

My Favorite Foods
by Remayja

1. pizza

2. apples

3. yogurt

4. cheeseburgers

5. macaroni and cheese

Magic Words

This word activity is fun to do anytime with your class, but it is especially fun to do around Halloween.

1. Using a white crayon, write secret words on white pieces of paper (one or two words per sheet). You can put the same word or different words on each paper. You may also want to draw a simple picture to accompany each word.
2. Have children take turns coming up to a painting station and selecting a piece of paper.
3. Have them place the papers on easels or on a table and cover them with a black paint wash (diluted tempera paint). Magically, the words will pop out of the black background.
4. Have children bring their dried papers to circle time and discuss their secret word or words.

Pumpkin Words

A tidy assortment of pumpkins can be an unusual source of seasonal words.

1. Use permanent markers to write seasonal words on a variety of pumpkins.
2. Place the pumpkins in your writing center so children can refer to them when writing.

Variation: If your school has a gardening spot, plant pumpkin seeds during the summer. While the pumpkins are still small, use a nail to etch a word in each one. Children will delight in watching the words grow along with the pumpkins.

Thankful Words

Thanksgiving offers a perfect opportunity to display meaningful words.

1. Create a turkey body and head out of construction paper and attach it to a bulletin board or wall.
2. Cut out large paper feathers using different fall colors. Make one feather per child.
3. Have each child come up, one at a time, and tell something that she is thankful for.
4. Write her answer on a feather and let her place it on the turkey.
5. At circle time, discuss Thanksgiving and all the things that people are thankful for; then let each child read her feather to the class.

Turkey Words

Trim a turkey with functional feathers!

1. Cut a large turkey body shape from brown bulletin board paper. Add features.
2. Choose a word you want to emphasize, such as *thanks.*
3. Cut out some feather shapes from colorful construction paper and program each with a letter to make the word. Arrange them in an arc on a bulletin board.
4. Mount the turkey shape in front of the feathers, with the feathers sticking out behind the turkey body.
5. Display the turkey for a few days; then replace the existing word with a new seasonal word spelled out in turkey feathers.

Christmas Balls

Whether or not you have a Christmas tree in your classroom, this is a great present to make for your children.

1. Purchase inexpensive, unbreakable Christmas balls, and write each child's name on one with glitter glue.
2. Hang the balls up in your room for everyone to see and read. Then wrap them up in tissue paper and let your children take them home as a gift from you.

Surprise Boxes

You will need a collection of small decorative boxes for this activity.

1. Place several small boxes on a table.
2. Put an alphabet letter manipulative inside each box.
3. Encourage your children to look inside each box and name the letter.
4. Have your students practice writing the letters they see.
5. Change the letters frequently so that each time a child peeks into the boxes, she sees different letters.

Valentine Words

The days leading up to Valentine's Day are great times for children to be surrounded by meaningful words. Try this fun game with your children.

1. Sort out matching pairs of valentines from a boxed set. Make sure you don't have any duplicate pairs. Divide them into two identical piles. Put one pile into a bag.
2. Have your children sit in a circle.
3. Keep the bag of cards and give each youngster a card from the pile. If you have any leftover cards, be sure to remove their matches from your bag.
4. Draw one card from your bag.
5. Read the card aloud, but do not turn it around to show the picture.
6. Have students try to recognize the words on their cards to see who has the matching card.
7. If the child cannot identify his card, show your card so he can find the match by looking at the picture.

Extension: Mix up all the cards. Place them on a table and let your children take turns sorting the cards into matching pairs.

Valentine Rubbings

Here is a fun way for nonwriters to make valentines with sayings on them.

1. Glue large heart-shaped doilies on 8" x 11" pieces of poster board.
2. Using glue, write short valentine sayings on the doilies. Place them in a center when dry, along with stickers, markers, white paper, and unwrapped crayons.
3. When a child wants to make a valentine, he reads and chooses a saying, then makes a rubbing of the saying and the outline of the heart shape.
4. Encourage him to embellish the rubbing using the available supplies.
5. Have the child sign his name at the bottom of the rubbing and give the valentine to a friend or loved one.

Examples of valentine sayings: Hugs, Kisses, I Love You!, Be Mine!, Hug Me!

Word Eggs

These paper eggs will come in handy for a number of different activities.

1. Cut out a supply of white paper eggs.
2. Write the same word on each of a pair of eggs with a white crayon to make several sets.
3. Mix up the eggs and place them in your art area.
4. Have each child paint one or two eggs with Easter egg dye.
5. When the eggs are dry, use them to play a matching game.

Variations:

• Write names on the eggs and let your children take turns delivering them.
• Write one word of a spring sentence on each egg and attach the eggs to a wall out of order to make a surprise sentence for your children to figure out. Example: "The Easter Bunny likes to paint eggs."

You are special!

Affirmation Eggs

These affirmations are sure to make your little ones feel special.

1. Cut a class supply of 1" x 2" strips of white paper.
2. On each strip, write a short affirmation telling a child how special he is. Examples:
   • You are special!
   • You are the best!
   • Wow! What a kid!
   • You are great!
   • You have a sunny smile!
3. Place the strips inside small plastic eggs.
4. Place the eggs in a basket.
5. Have each child come up and choose an egg.
6. Have each child open his egg; then help him read the message aloud. Allow children to take the eggs home, or keep them in your classroom to use again.

Variation: Use the same eggs and write action words on the strips. Have children take turns drawing an egg, reading it with you, and then acting out the action for the other children to guess.

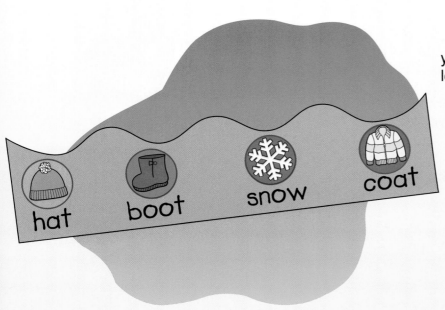

Bulletin Board Trim

Add personal or seasonal touches to your bulletin board trims for a fresh new look.

- Before mounting plain-colored trim around bulletin boards or wall areas, write simple seasonal words on it.
- Decorate the trim by attaching seasonal stickers and then writing the corresponding word near each sticker as shown.
- At the beginning of the year, write each student's name on trim and place it around your classroom door or a welcome bulletin board.

Seasonal Word Charts

Seasonal word charts reinforce meaningful words for young children.

1. Write out four to six common words associated with the current season on large chart paper.
2. Draw a picture next to each word.
3. Have each child pick an object on the chart and then draw a picture of it and dictate a word or sentence about it.
4. Make a new word chart to post each season.

Extension: You can play a riddle game by making up a riddle for a picture on the chart for students to solve.

Example: Sun
   It is something that glows in the sky.
   It is bright.
   It gives us heat.
   What is it?

Room Signs

Go a step beyond ordinary labeling of classroom areas. Encourage your children to notice the special characteristics of each written word while participating in this activity.

1. Label index cards to match your classroom signs. You'll need at least one card per child.
2. At circle time, pass out the area cards.
3. Have children read their cards and go to the areas with the matching word signs. Provide assistance as necessary, helping children confirm their conclusions by matching the shapes of the letters on their cards to the ones on the signs.

Signs and More

As interest develops in center-related play, have children assist you in labeling objects and making provisions for related reading and writing opportunities.

- Housekeeping Area
    Cooking charts
    Shopping lists
    Phone lists
    Food boxes with words
    Restaurant name banners
- Block Area
    Signs for community buildings
- Science Area
    Labels for collections
    Texture words
    Opposite words (such as *light* and *heavy*)
- Music Area
    Instrument labels
    Headphone and tape area labels
    Recorder labels
- Art Area
    Collage box labels
    Label for art materials on counters or shelves
- Display Area
    Collections of toys with words on them, such as bears that have words on their shirts.

Room Labels

Play a word game with your children, usings labels of classroom objects and matching word cards.

1. Program index cards with words identical to those on labeled classroom objects (such as *chair, table,* or *cubbies*) and put them in a bag.
2. At circle time, have each youngster reach into the bag and draw a label.
3. Have each child go in search of the label that matches his word card.
4. When each child knows what his word card says, he returns to the circle.
5. Have each child take a turn holding up his word card and reading it.

More Environmental Signs

Both inside and outside your classroom, there are numerous areas to post word signs. As natural opportunities arise, call children's attention to a label or two and discuss the word, its beginning sound, or its beginning letter.

- Hang an "in use/not in use" sign outside your class restroom.
- Post exit signs.
- If you have double doors, label one "in" and one "out."
- Post the word "water" over the water fountain.
- Outside, post signs that say "one way" or "stop" on paths where children ride tricycles.
- If you have a garden area, put up lots of signs naming what you have planted.
- Put signs such as "swing" and "slide" on play equipment, and post direction signs that read "up" and "down."

Class Jobs

Here is an easy idea for a print-rich job chart.
1. Hang up a pocket chart.
2. Cut job cards to fit the pockets.
3. On each card, write the word for the job and put a small picture of it underneath.
4. Place the job cards in the pockets on the left-hand side.
5. Make a set of name cards for your children.
6. Place one or more names in the pocket to the right of each job.
7. When it's time for a particular job to be done, have a child refer to the chart to confirm whose job it is.

Variation: Occasionally let your children help you determine job helpers with this simple activity.
1. Turn the job cards facedown on a table and mix them up.
2. Have each child take a turn choosing a card.
3. Have each child place his job card in the pocket chart, along with his name card.

Birthday Books

Take advantage of children's birthdays to provide reading and writing opportunities related to the birthday child.
1. Prepare a birthday book for each child by printing statements (as shown) on individual pages. Then staple the pages together.
2. A few days before a child's birthday, give him a birthday book to take home and fill out.
3. Have the child bring the book back to the classroom on his birthday to share with the other children.
4. Leave the books in your reading area for everyone to enjoy.

Variation: Instead of birthday books, you can have children make a book about themselves the first week of school. Then have the books available for everyone to read throughout the year.

flower

cake

dog

Picture Gallery

Decorate your walls with pictures and print.
1. Look for magazine pictures or old photos that depict simple items, such as dogs, flowers, mountains, and lakes.
2. Glue each picture to a separate card and label it.
3. Encourage your children to bring in pictures to add to your gallery and have them suggest how to spell the words.
4. Encourage your children to read the words in your picture gallery during transition times.

Extension: If you get too many pictures, take some down and let your children help you sort them into categories. A few category suggestions are
- words that start with the designated sounds
- animals, people, and objects
- natural or man-made items

Familiar Signs

Take advantage of familiar logos by incorporating them into your picture gallery and throughout the classroom.
1. Display pictures of trademarked logos and road signs.
2. Make play menus with pictures of familiar restaurants on the covers for your children to use in restaurant role-playing.

stop

cereal

Event Albums

Highlight special events with these albums!

1. Whenever you have an event or special outing at your school, take pictures.
2. Place the photos in a photo album with simple, descriptive sentences placed under each picture.
3. Add to the album throughout the year.

Note: Keep your albums from year to year for students to read. Use the previous year's album to introduce future outings to the next class.

Word Mobiles

Don't forget about utilizing your classroom's overhead space for word mobiles. Make simple mobiles from rods or coat hangers. Suspend pictures and words about things you are studying.

- Seasonal Mobile: Suspend a seasonal word such as *Fall, Winter, Spring,* or *Summer,* and then suspend from it symbols of the season.
- Birthday Mobile: Suspend a large cardboard birthday cake with the month written on it. From that, suspend the names of children who have birthdays that month.
- Color Mobile: Suspend a large cardboard rainbow. From that, suspend colored paper shapes with the color words printed on them.

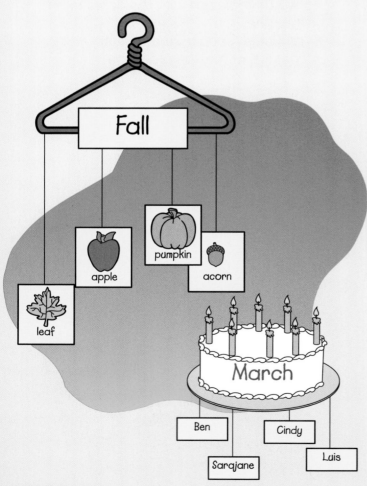

Motivational Stamps or Stickers

Besides rewarding children for hard work, "good job" stamps or stickers also help children learn to recognize new words.

- For younger children, look for stamps that say only one word.
  - Wow
  - Cool
  - Great
  - Super
  - Good
- For older children, look for stamps with harder words or two words.
  - Bravo
  - Terrific
  - Fantastic
  - Good Work
  - Super Job
  - Superstar
  - Well done

Tickets, Order Forms, and Checks

Stock your classroom with opportunities for meaningful reading and writing. Make tickets and order forms for children to use in their dramatic play.

- Train Tickets: Make tickets (approximately 2" x 3") and write the names of familiar cities on them. Keep them in a basket with a train conductor's hat.
- Parking Tickets: Make blank parking tickets for your children to use. Place them in a basket along with a police officer's hat.
- Order Pads: Make restaurant order pads with names of common foods. Place these in a basket with a checkered tablecloth, plastic tableware, and napkins.
- Checks: Make checks for your children to use while banking or shopping. Place them in a basket with a wallet and a purse.

Surveys

Weekly surveys are great opportunities for using both pictures and print.

1. Choose a survey topic, such as pets owned, eye color, or favorites (foods, sports, music, etc.).
2. Section chart paper into columns.
3. Have children help you determine column headings. Add related rebus drawings.
4. Survey each child and represent his response on the chart by writing his name.
5. Have children help you determine the column totals. Then review the chart together and discuss the information it represents.

Pets			
Danny	Julie		
Josh	Alvin		Ben
Michele	Jackson		Leah
Brian	José	Sara	Shemika
Nicki	Mia	John	Bonnie
dog	cat	fish	other or none

Reading Materials

Fill your classroom with a wide range of reading materials. Make sure your selections include topics and themes of interest to your students.

- Set up a special reading area in your room stocked with a generous assortment of children's books. Include dictionaries, story books, science books, holiday books, etc.
- Look for appropriate magazines for children, especially ones about young children or animals.
- Don't forget newspapers. Smaller weekly papers are easier for young children.

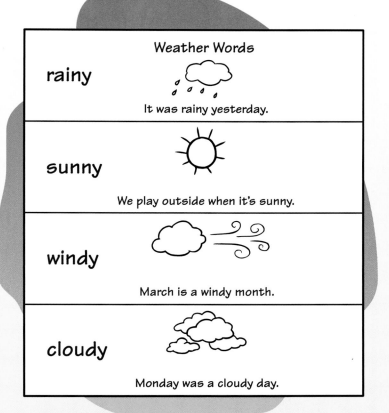

Weather Words

rainy	It was rainy yesterday.
sunny	We play outside when it's sunny.
windy	March is a windy month.
cloudy	Monday was a cloudy day.

Weather Words

Make a weather word chart for your classroom. Display it when you are studying weather, or if you have room, post it permanently.

1. Using a large marker, print the following weather words on your poster board: *rainy, sunny, windy, cloudy, snowy.*
2. Next to each word draw a simple picture depicting that type of weather.
3. Enlist student help to write a simple sentence about each type of weather.

Weather Songs

Take advantage of the chart from the activity above and use it at music time to sing about the current weather conditions with your children.

Rainy
(sung to the tune of "Bingo")

There was a farmer looked outside
And saw that it was rainy.
R-a-i-n-y, r-a-i-n-y, r-a-i-n-y.
He saw that it was rainy.

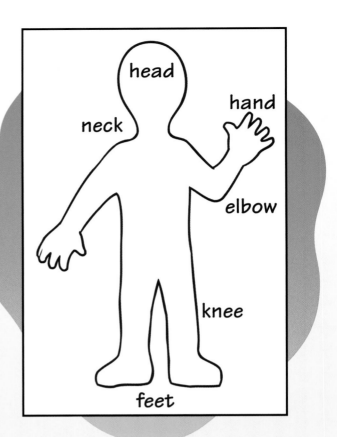

Body Part Words

Encourage your children to learn to recognize words for familiar parts of their bodies with this simple chart.

1. Make a large body chart by drawing around a child on a large piece of bulletin board paper.
2. Write the words *head* and *feet* on the outline in their proper locations.
3. Encourage students to read the words and point to their related body parts.
4. Each week, add two more body part words.
5. Continue while interest lasts.

Body Chart Game

Here is a fun game to play with your youngsters when the body chart from the activity above contains four or more words.

1. Place the body chart on the floor.
2. Set out two beanbags.
3. Have your children take turns tossing the beanbags onto the chart.
4. Give each child two tosses (if necessary) to land on a body part that is marked.
5. Ask him to name the body part. Guide him in observing something about the written word (for example, *head* begins with *h*).
6. Tell him to point to his corresponding body part and encourage his classmates to do the same.
7. Continue playing until each child has taken a turn.

Reading Wall

Children will enjoy decorating a classroom wall with their favorite words.

1. Put up a large piece of paper on the wall.
2. Ask your children to bring in words they can read. These words can be written by a parent or cut from magazines, cereal boxes, etc.
3. Have them tape or glue the words to the paper.
4. When a child adds a word, have her read the word to the class.
5. Occasionally, point to the words on this special word wall and have youngsters read them aloud.
6. If students have trouble reading a word, provide assistance.

Classroom Posters

Interesting pictures from magazines are sure to spark interest in reading and writing.

1. Cut out a large ad or article picture from a magazine. Choose one that has something funny or unusual happening in it.
2. Glue the picture onto a piece of 9" x 12" construction paper.
3. Hang the picture in your classroom.
4. After a few days, tape the picture onto a larger, lined sheet of paper.
5. Ask your children what they think the picture is about.
6. Write their comments on the paper under the picture in simple sentences.
7. Read their comments aloud.
8. Leave the poster up for a week and encourage your children to read the comments under the picture.
9. Repeat the process with a different picture.

Wow! This is a little car!
I want a van.
I'm squished.
I'm going to the grocery store.

Word Bracelets

What's the word? Create word bracelets to call attention to words from a story or to introduce word clues about an impending surprise.

1. Provide a 1" x 6" strip of lightweight tagboard for each child.
2. Write a special word in the center of each strip. Strips can all have the same word, or they can have different words.
3. Give each child a word strip.
4. Explain her word and use it in a sentence for her.
5. Help her turn the strip into a bracelet by taping the ends together.
6. Invite her to wear her word bracelet for the rest of the day.

Parting Messages

Send children on word hunts at home!

1. On a small index card, write a word with which you want a student to become familiar.
2. Place the card in a small envelope.
3. Have each child take his envelope home and use the card to find the word. Instruct him to cut out a sample of the word and bring it back to school in his envelope.

Tips for this activity:

- Use simple words like *the, cereal, drink,* and *red.*
- Use seasonal words like *hot, cold, snow,* and *rain.*
- Be sure to use words that can be easily found in newspapers, magazines, labels, and packaging around the home.

Word Collections

Encourage your children to create word collections.

1. Set out a supply of index cards cut in half.
2. When a child discovers a special word that she wants in her collection, she brings you a card on which to write the word. (You may want to limit each student to one word per day or week.)
3. When a child has a small collection, ask her to read the words to you.
4. Remove words that become less important to a child.

Systems for keeping word collections:
- Punch a hole in the top corner of each word card and have your children add the cards to metal rings or other fastening devices.
- Purchase plastic ID holders in which your children can store their cards.
- Give each child a sturdy envelope in which to keep her cards.

Favorites Chart

Pick a category and have each child make a small word chart.

1. Select a category that is meaningful to your students, such as favorite foods, favorite toys, or favorite games.
2. Sit with each child at a table.
3. Using a 12" x 18" piece of construction paper, write the category and the student's name at the top of her chart as shown.
4. Ask her to tell you her five favorite items in this category.
5. List the child's favorite things on her chart and discuss different aspects of the printed words (such as the beginning letters).
6. Let the children decorate their charts with crayons or markers.
7. Store the charts at your writing center and remind children to refer to their charts as they write.

Stamp Books

Children will launch into this stamping project with a lot of energy. Afterward they'll all have booklets they can enthusiastically read.

1. Set out one kind of stamp and an ink pad.
2. Set out sheets of copy paper on which you have written the corresponding word.
3. Have each child take a turn stamping a page with images.
4. Discuss the word and its meaning with each child, label his page with his name, and store his page for later use.
5. In the days that follow, repeat this activity several times using other kinds of stamps (cats, bugs, etc.).
6. Collate each child's pages and staple them together to create a booklet he'll be eager to read.

Sentence-Starter Stamps

These rubber stamps will prompt plenty of creative writing.

1. Have rubber stamps made for your classroom that say, in large print, things like "My favorite food is…," "I like to…," and "Winter is…."
2. Introduce one of these stamps to your youngsters, familiarizing them with the words and the incomplete thought.
3. Talk about several different ways to finish the sentence.
4. Place the stamp in a writing center along with ink pads and a variety of writing supplies.
5. Invite children to stamp the incomplete thought on paper and draw and/or write to complete the thought.
6. At circle time, invite children to share their writing with their classmates.

Note: If stamps are not available, use a computer to print the desired phrase in advance; then make a class supply to place in your writing center.

Stories and Games

This section consists of:

- ideas to get children involved in crafting stories and songs

- word-oriented games to make learning and reading words fun

- ideas to reinforce color words and other high-frequency words

Bag Stories

This fun, word-oriented storytime activity is geared for student participation.

1. Print a number of words on index cards. Include words that all begin with the same sound and letter or words that share a common theme.
2. Place the cards in a bag.
3. At storytime, hold up the bag and tell your children that the bag contains some story words.
4. Have your children take turns drawing words that you will incorporate into an impromptu story.
5. When a word is drawn from the bag, read it with the child's assistance. Have him momentarily hold it up while you incorporate the word in a sentence for your story.
6. Continue telling the story until everyone has had a turn to draw and add a word.

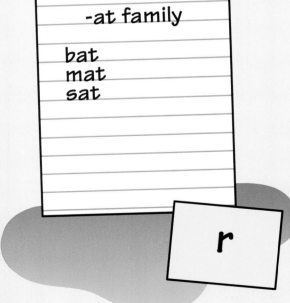

Word Family Stories

Involve students in this word family activity.

1. On each of several small index cards, print a desired lowercase letter. (Based on the word family you choose, you will want to select appropriate letters.)
2. Place the letter cards inside a bag.
3. Tape a lined piece of chart paper to the wall.
4. At the top of the paper, write "[-at] family."
5. Have a child draw a letter card from the bag.
6. Have him hold up the letter drawn and place it on the chart to the left of the rime. Then have everyone help decide what the word is.
7. Write the word on your chart.
8. With student help, start a story using the word.
9. Repeat until your letter supply is exhausted or each child has had a turn to draw a letter, make a word, and incorporate it into the story.

   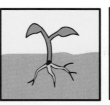  

| Here is a seed. | I planted it in the dirt. | It grew. | It grew more. | It got big! | The flower is pretty. |

Wordless Stories

Wordless stories can be used to help children learn how to read and write.

1. Buy two copies of a wordless storybook.
2. Cut the pages out of the two books and use them to create one complete story by taping the pages in sequence on a wall.
3. Under each page, tape some white paper strips.
4. At storytime, ask your children to tell you the story.
5. Write the story in their words on the paper strips.
6. Encourage your children to read the story on their own or to ask an adult to read it to them.
7. If desired, replace the story strips with blank ones and repeat the process for a new version of the story.

Wordless Comics

Use favorite childhood comics to create simple, meaningful stories.

1. Look through the comics in a newspaper.
2. Choose a short, wordless comic (or mask text from a scripted strip).
3. Cut it out and glue each section near the top of a separate piece of lined paper.
4. At storytime, hold up the first section of the cartoon and ask your children, "What is happening in this picture?"
5. Write a simple version of what they say on the lined paper.
6. Read the caption aloud.
7. Repeat this process with other sections of the cartoon, and end with a reading of the entire retelling.
8. For repeated readings, sequence the pages and staple them between construction paper covers.

The dog saw the birthday cake. He wanted to eat it all up!

Story Charts

These repetitious rebus charts are guaranteed to inspire reading practice, so be sure to rotate them often.

1. Pick out a simple phrase that you can repeat in a story.
2. Write a short introductory sentence; then write the chosen sentence three to six times on chart paper.
3. Title the story.
4. Have your children help you create the story by drawing a picture of an object to complete each sentence. Tape the pictures to the chart.
5. With student help, write a short sentence to conclude the story.
6. Read the story aloud. After you have read the story this way for a while, add the words for the pictures on strips of paper taped below the pictures. Reread the story, referring to the newly added words.

Rebus Farm Story

E-I-E-I-O! Here is a simple farm rebus that's just right for reading.

1. At the top of a piece of poster board, write the title "Animal Talk."
2. Below the title, write a short introductory sentence. Follow it with sentences about farm animals and the sounds they make.
   Sentence suggestions:
   The _____ says, "Quack."
   The _____ says, "Moo."
   The _____ says, "Woof."
   The _____ says, "Neigh."
3. Have youngsters draw pictures of animals to place on the lines.
4. Write a concluding sentence together. Read the story aloud.
5. When students are familiar with the story, have them help you replace the pictures with animal name labels.

I am red.
I have a ladder.
I help put out fires.
What am I?

Riddle Stories

Solving riddles is a fun way to reinforce reading and writing skills. Try it!

1. Make up simple riddles for your children to read.
2. Point to each word as you read the riddle.
3. Discuss items that fit the descriptions.

Examples:
I am red.
I am round.
I grow on a tree.
What am I?

I am red.
I have a ladder.
I help put out fires.
What am I?

Word Cube Stories

A plastic photo cube or a square tissue box is the key to this activity.

1. Write six story words on cards cut to the size of the cube or box.
2. Attach them to your cube.
3. Have children in a small group take turns rolling the word cube.
4. Help them incorporate each word they roll into a sentence that becomes part of a story.

End-of-Day Activity Lists

This activity will convey to your children that words and sentences have meaning and are often about common things.

1. At the end of the day, gather your children and ask them what they enjoyed the most that day.
2. On a large sheet of paper, jot down their comments using simple sentences.
3. Read the list to your children, pointing to each word as you read it. Display the list.
4. The following day, encourage children to read the list to review what they did the day before.

Monday, January 19

We went to art today.

There were corn dogs for lunch.

We made patterns.

We got a new printer!

Today's Lunch Menu

carrots
and apples

Menu Charts

It's never too early to think about the day's lunch menu, and this activity provides a helping of reading practice!

1. Post a daily lunch menu (the larger the better) in your room.
2. Encourage your children to use letter-sound associations to try to figure out what they will be having to eat that day.

Baa, baa black _____
Have you any wool?

Baa, baa black sheep
Have you any wool?
Yes sir, yes sir,
Three bags full.

Sheep!

Song and Rhyme Charts

Familiar songs and rhymes are easier for your children to read.

1. On large chart tablets, write short familiar rhymes for your students to read.
2. Every day, for several days, read a rhyme aloud. Point to each word as you read. After a while omit a word and see if your students can fill in the word you missed.
3. Periodically add some new rhymes.

Extension: Point out which words rhyme.

Open-Ended Songs

A sing-along is a fine excuse for reading fun!

1. Make a song chart with a song that is open ended, such as "Old MacDonald."
2. Leave spaces where animals are named and where the sounds belong.
3. Make a set of animal cards with both pictures and words.
4. Let children take turns choosing cards.
5. Have a child hold up her card and name the animal.
6. Have everyone read the song, adding the name of the animal that was drawn and the sound it makes.
7. Every now and then, sing the song with your little ones, pointing to the words (or having a child point) as you sing.

horse

sheep

pig

Sentence Strips

Grab some sentence strips and a pocket chart for this fun activity.

1. Color and cut out selected picture cards from pages 220–224.
2. Write on three strips simple, incomplete sentences to correspond with the pictures.
3. Have children take turns reading the sentences and choosing a picture to put into the sentence. Accept all answers, even if they are silly.

I see a dancing kite!

Story Strips

In this game, children will recall a story and then find the correct word to finish the sentence.

1. Pick a sentence from a story you have just read. Write it on sentence strips in an incomplete form.
2. Place the strips in a pocket chart.
3. On each of three cards, write words that might complete the sentence.
4. Have your children choose the correct word to finish the sentence.
5. Read the sentence with your students. Repeat this sequence with other sentences and words.

Opposites

This versatile activity can be used for several pairs of opposites. Just replace the signs so students practice reading high/low, in/out, up/down, over/under, and so forth.

1. Cut out two tagboard signs for this game. On one sign, write "high." On the other write "low."
2. Invite each child to take a turn holding and reading the signs.
3. Go around your room and point to objects that are obviously high or low.
4. Have the child hold up the sign that describes the object's location.

Color Words

Your students will enjoy this simple color word game.

1. Cut out two signs.
2. Print a different color name on each sign.
3. Have children take turns going around the room and pointing to objects that match each color word.

139

Racing Families

This word-family writing game will have your little ones cruising into reading!

1. Give each child a small chalkboard and a piece of chalk.
2. Write a word-family ending on your chalkboard.
3. Set a timer for two minutes and have each child use that time to write as many words (both real and nonsense) as possible that fit the word family.
4. When the time is up, discuss the words and decide which are real and which are nonsense.
5. Make a master chart of all the real words. Put it in your writing center.

Flash!

Youngsters are sure to get fired up about reading sight words when they play this card game!

1. Write on index cards common words that your students are learning to read.
2. On two cards, draw a burst and write "flash!"
3. Put all the cards in a bag.
4. Have a pair of students take turns drawing and reading cards.
5. If a child reads the word correctly, he keeps the card. If he does not read the card correctly, he puts it back in the bag.
6. If a child draws a "flash!" card, he puts all of his cards back in the bag.
7. The winner is the player with more cards at the end of a specified time period.

Pocket Chart Matchup

Whenever children pass by this pocket chart, they'll be eager to show off their reading skills.

1. Prepare several sets of three consonant-vowel-consonant word cards (each having a different beginning letter), along with three picture cards that match the words. (If desired, use selected picture cards from pages 220–224.)
2. Display one set of three picture cards along the left margin of the pocket chart. Place the matching word cards in random order elsewhere in the chart.
3. During transition or center time, encourage children who pass by the chart to match the word cards to the pictures. Demonstrate how this can be done by recalling the sound the word's first letter makes.
4. Discuss the matches the children make. When matches are correct, have the children who made the matches explain to their classmates how they did it.
5. Once three matches have been made, return the cards to random locations for repeated use.
6. Rotate sets of three cards for variety.

Word Mats

Each month provides a fabulous new opportunity to introduce seasonal or thematic words.

1. To prepare a word mat, write four or five seasonal or thematic words on a sheet of paper. Make a construction paper copy for each child.
2. Read the words to children as they locate them on their copies.
3. Provide art supplies and have children decorate the mats and label them with their names.
4. When the mats are dry, laminate them or cover them with clear Con-Tact covering.
5. Throughout the month, use the mats as workmats or placemats and informally call attention to the words or letters on them.

Extension: Play this fun game using your word mats (above) while your children are waiting for their lunch.

1. Say one of the words on the mats.
2. Have each child find the word and place his finger on it.
3. Continue by having students find another word.
4. Encourage them to share how they recognized the word.

Action-Word Game

This is a great word game to get children moving.

1. Make a set of cards with action words on them, such as *sneak, jump, skip,* or *bend.*
2. Place the cards in a bag.
3. Have each child take a turn drawing a card.
4. Read the word with the child.
5. Have him act out the word without disclosing it to his classmates.
6. Have the other children try to guess the word.

jump

My Action Book

Takisha

running

jumping

Action-Word Picture Book

This book is lots of fun to make and even more fun to share with families.

1. On each of five sheets of paper, write an action word, such as *running, jumping, swimming, climbing,* or *crawling.*
2. Make a cover page that says "My Action Book."
3. Make each child a copy of the cover and pages. With the cover on top, staple the pages together.
4. Pass out the booklets and go through them with your students, reading each page aloud.
5. During the next week, have children illustrate the pages in their books. Encourage them to ask you if they are unsure about what a page says.
6. Let your children take their books home to read to their families.

corn

sugar

salt

wheat

Searching for Sugar

The great thing about this game is that it teaches word recognition in a familiar setting.

1. Set up a mini grocery store in your classroom that has lots of empty food boxes (especially cereal) and some cans of fruits and vegetables.
2. Set out a small recipe box that contains cards bearing simple words that might be found on containers of food. Make duplicate cards for some words.
3. To play the game, each child goes to the box and draws a card.
4. She searches the food containers until she finds one that contains the word on the card.
5. She sets the container and the card on a special shelf. No one else can use that card or that container for the rest of the day.
6. Near the end of each day, have each child take a turn showing classmates the matches she found. Then return the cards and the boxes to the grocery store area.

Mystery-Word Search

This game offers letter recognition and word formation opportunities.

1. For this activity, choose a word that is already posted in the classroom. Write each of its letters on a separate index card.
2. Hide the letter cards around the room where the children will find them throughout the day.
3. When all the letters have been found, have the children work with you to arrange the letters to spell a word. Tape the letters together on a paper strip.
4. Discuss the word, its meaning, and any observations children make about it, such as the letter sounds it begins and ends with.
5. Encourage children to find a word posted in the classroom that matches the word.

clock

Floor Words

Create a stir about a word that's central to the season, a current theme, or a special story.

1. Using masking tape, write a word in large letters on your classroom floor.
2. Let your children walk around it, play on it, drive cars on it, lie on it, etc.
3. When children ask what the word is, have them help you figure it out using letter-sound association.
4. During the next few days, whenever that word comes up in conversation, direct children's attention back to the taped word.

Word Walk

Play this game outside on a sidewalk or other paved area.

1. Before children go outside, write a few words in large letters with chalk on a sidewalk or other paved area. Choose from these words: *tree, free, flee,* or *free*. (You may substitute other words from a rhyming set, modifying the rhyme as necessary for shorter words such as *me, be*, and *we*.)
2. Have your children walk around a word and repeat the rhyme below (inserting appropriate letters as the word dictates).

> Round and round and round we go.
> Here is a word we don't know.
> First a(n) [E],
> Then an [R],
> Then an [E] and an [E].
> Round and round and round we go.
> What can this word be?

3. Choose a child to go in the middle of the circle and stand on the first letter. Have her say the letter's sound. (Provide assistance as necessary.)
4. Continue having students give a sound for each letter.
5. Have the children say their sounds, one after the other, until someone blends the sounds and says the word.

Color Puzzles

This can be a great getting-acquainted game as well as a word recognition game.

1. On colorful tagboard shapes, write the corresponding color words in large print. (Create enough shapes so that there is one for every two students in your class.)
2. Cut each card into two pieces and mix them all together.
3. Pass out the pieces so that each child receives one.
4. Have your children search the room, find their color partners, and sit down together.
5. Have each pair complete its puzzle and then read its word aloud for the class.

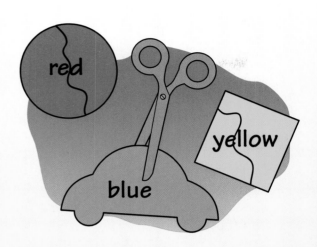

Color Trail Game

After you have introduced this color trail game to the whole group, it can be played by two, three, or four children during center time.

1. Cut out and laminate two construction paper squares in each of the following colors: black, blue, brown, green, orange, purple, red, and yellow. Also make one white square that says "Finish." Create 16 word cards labeled with the color words listed (two per color).
2. Gather colored plastic bowling pins or beanbags to use as game markers.
3. Tape the squares to the floor to form a color trail in an area of your room. Place the squares so that the eight basic colors appear in a pattern and the trail ends with the Finish square.
4. Place the deck of color word cards facedown in the playing area. (The first few times children play this game you may want to include only two or three different color words and then gradually add other color words.)
5. Have each player, in turn, draw a card, read it (checking with other children and a color word wall display if necessary to confirm the color word), and place his marker on the next space on the trail that contains that color.
6. Play continues in this manner until a child reaches the Finish square.

Variation: Revise the trail to show a numeral on each square, and supply a deck of number word cards.

Colors Abound

Colors and color words abound in this circle-time activity.

1. For each child, provide a color-coded word card.
2. Ask each child to find a small object that's the same color as his color word card, and have him join his classmates at the circle when he has found one.
3. Have each child, in turn, hold up his color word card, read it, and tell about the matching object.

Word Erase

You will need a chalkboard or a dry-erase board for this activity.

1. On a board, write five or six words your children are familiar with.
2. Have each child, in turn, come to the board and read a word.
3. If the child can read the word correctly, he gets to erase the word. If he needs assistance reading, provide help and then have him read the word and erase it.
4. As words are erased, add more words so that each child gets a turn.

Fishing for Words

You could fill a pond with all the words your children love to use, and in this idea you do!

1. Make a few simple fishing poles out of wooden dowels, yarn, and circular magnets.
2. Look through recent stories that children have dictated to you. Write simple words from those stories on fish-shaped cutouts.
3. Attach a paper clip to the mouth area of each fish before placing all the fish facedown on a paper pond cutout.
4. Have children take turns fishing and then reading the words on the fish they catch.

Word Concentration Game

This game should be played with a small group of children on the floor or at a table. It is great for developing memory skills as well as reading skills.

1. On each of six 3" x 5" index cards, write a different word. Make a duplicate set of the cards.
2. Mix up the cards.
3. Lay them facedown on a table in two or three rows.
4. Playing in pairs, one child turns over two cards.
5. If the cards match, he must say the word before keeping the two cards. (Provide assistance as needed.)
6. If the cards don't match, he returns them to their original positions.
7. Play continues with the second child taking a turn.
8. The game ends when all of the cards have been paired and their words read.

Word Trains

Choo! Choo! This game, played like dominoes, has children adding to a long train of matching words.

1. Using a marker, divide each of 21 small index cards in half.
2. On each card, write two different animal names. The following work well: *dog, cat, bird, pig, fish.*
3. Have three or four players sit on the floor. Give each player three cards.
4. Put the remaining cards facedown in a pile.
5. Draw a card to use as the starting point; then give the first player the opportunity to place one of his cards with a matching word next to the card. He may continue to lay down cards as long as he has matches. If he has no match, he must take a card from the deck, and the turn passes to the next player.
6. Players take turns participating in this manner. The first child to play all of his cards wins the round.

Go Fish!

This card game makes your children's favorite words a splash of fun.

1. Label six index cards with different words your children already know how to read. Include pictures if desired.
2. Using the same words, label three more sets of cards for a total of 24.
3. Shuffle the cards and give four cards to each of four children.
4. Have each child check his cards for matching words.
5. During his turn, the first child lays down any matching pairs, then asks another player for a word card that matches one of his remaining cards. He should hold his card up for the others to see.
6. If the player gets another match, he lays down the pair. If he does not, the child of whom the card was requested says, "Go fish." The player must take a card from the deck.
7. Turns continue in this manner. The child with the most pairs when a player runs out of cards is the winner.

Go fish!

Writing Words

This section consists of ideas for:

- letter-sound correspondence
- letter formation
- concepts of print
- writing with all kinds of media

Fingerpaint Writing

Turn art time into writing time with this activity.

1. Give each child a sheet of fingerpaint paper.
2. Place one or two globs of fingerpaint on each paper.
3. Invite each child to fingerpaint for several minutes.
4. Show him how to clear his painting surface by rubbing the side of his hand across his paper to move the paint to the edge.
5. With a clean slate, encourage each youngster to practice writing letters or words with the paint.

Shaving Cream Writing

Your children will love the feel, fragrance, and colorful appeal of this activity.

1. Give each child a sheet of fingerpaint paper.
2. Squirt a glob of nonmenthol shaving cream in the middle of each student's paper.
3. Provide students with access to one or more salt shakers filled with powdered tempera paint.
4. Have each child sprinkle some paint on her shaving cream and then blend the two with her fingers.
5. Instruct her to smooth out the shaving cream with the side of her hand to create a thin layer.
6. Have her use the surface to write or copy her favorite words.

Spaghetti Words

Noodles wiggle and children giggle while forming words with this fun medium!

1. In giant letters, write a three- or four-letter word on each of four 12" x 18" sheets of poster board to make workmats.
2. Laminate the mats.
3. Cook some spaghetti according to package directions.
4. Drain the spaghetti and keep it covered until cool enough to handle.
5. Put the mats and the spaghetti at a center.
6. Have each child who visits the center choose a mat and then place noodles on the letters of the word.
7. When a child is finished and has shown you his work, discard the noodles on his mat and invite another child to visit the center.

Special Remembrance

Preserve a special school memory with these word rubbings.

1. After an exciting field trip or experience, have each child think of a word that reminds her of the event and explain why.
2. Write each child's word on a sheet of construction paper; then trace over the letters of each word with a trail of glue (from a squeeze bottle). Set the words aside to dry overnight.
3. The following day, have each child place a sheet of white paper over her word and use the side of a crayon to make a rubbing of it.
4. As the child dictates something about her memory of the event, write her thoughts on the rubbing. Encourage her to illustrate and write something else on her rubbing if she would like.
5. Place the programmed construction paper sheets in the writing center and remind children that they can refer to them when writing.

Punch Writing

This easy beginning-writing activity for young children will have them punching their way to letter formation.

1. Gather a class set of clean foam fruit or vegetable trays and coffee stirrers.
2. Write a letter or a short word on each tray.
3. Give each child a tray and a stirrer.
4. Have him use his stirrer to punch holes along the letter(s) on his tray.

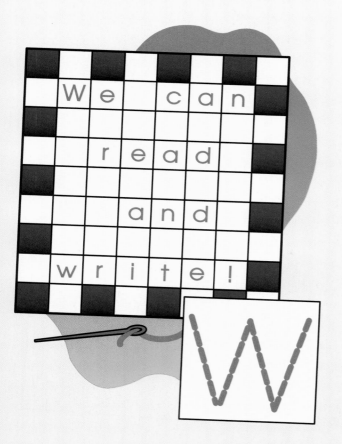

Sewing Words

Use this sewing activity to introduce letters or words. You will need burlap, four embroidery hoops, 18" lengths of yarn (one for each child), a marker, and four plastic sewing needles.

1. Cut the burlap into 9" x 9" squares.
2. Use a marker to write a letter or word on each square.
3. Working with a group of four students, place a burlap square in each hoop and then give one to each child.
4. For each student, thread a needle with yarn and tie a knot in one end.
5. Have each youngster sew along the lines of her letter or word.

Extension: When arranged together on a bulletin board or sewn with other squares, these letters can create a quiltlike message your students will love to read.

Sand Table Writing

Turn your sand table into a writing surface.

1. Remove any play items from your sand table.
2. Cut out several cardboard rectangles.
3. Using the cardboard, have students help you smooth out the sand.
4. In turn, have each child write in the sand with his fingers or with a craft stick.
5. Post words or sentences students know near the sand table. Encourage youngsters to use these words as they write.

Salt Writing

These salt-writing lids are fun and help children develop coordination skills necessary for writing on paper.

1. Gather one or two sturdy box lids.
2. Pour enough salt into each lid to cover the bottom.
3. Put the lids in a center.
4. Encourage a student visiting the center to use her finger to write letters or short words in the salt. Provide models of some current vocabulary words.
5. To start over, have the child gently shake the lid from side to side to make a clean slate on which to write.

Writing Center

A wonderful way to encourage writing in your preschool or kindergarten classroom is to stock a writing center with writing utensils and office supplies. Consider some or all of these for your writing center:

- paper (plain, lined, and decorative)
- pencils, pens, and markers
- notebooks
- clipboards
- blank books
- recipe boxes and cards
- letter stencils and tracing sheets
- sandpaper letters
- letter stamps
- letter-writing practice sheets
- children's dictionaries
- small chalkboards and chalk
- magnetic board and letters

Mail Center

Mail call! Next to your writing center, why not create a classroom post office. Stock it with the following:

- rubber office stamps and stamp pads
- stationery and cards
- different-size envelopes
- stamps or stickers
- computer labels
- junk mail
- phone books
- catalogs
- mailbox or individual student mailboxes

Tracing Papers

These reusable tracing sheets are easy to make and can be used year after year.

1. Use a highlighter to write letters or words on writing paper.
2. Laminate the sheets or cover them with clear Con-Tact covering.
3. Put the tracing sheets, dry-erase markers, or some dark crayons (test the crayons—some colors work better than others), and paper towels at a center.
4. Have each child trace the letters or words on his sheet with a crayon or marker.
5. When he has finished tracing, have him wipe the markings off the sheet with a paper towel.

Tracing Shadows

With a few magnetic letters and an overhead projector, youngsters are ready to trace words!

1. Use magnetic letters to form a word or several words on an overhead projector.
2. Project the word(s) onto a board.
3. In turn, have each child trace over the projected word(s).
4. When she has finished tracing, have her erase the board to ready it for the next student.

Writing With Chalk

Chalk and chalkboards have always been favorite writing tools with young children.

1. Stock your writing center with several small chalkboards, colorful chalk, and an eraser.
2. Program index cards with words you would like your students to practice writing.
3. In turn, have each child choose a card and write its word on a chalkboard.
4. After he has written several words, have him erase the board to ready it for the next student.

Road Words

Vroom, vroom! This activity is great for kinesthetic learners because it involves movement.

1. Use masking tape to form simple words in large letters on a floor.
2. To help teach students the proper way to write letters, put a green sticky dot where a letter begins and a red sticky dot where it ends.
3. Have each child use a toy car to drive over the words (roads), using the dots as a guide to make sure she forms the letters correctly.

Writing Practice Sheets

There are a number of simple reproducible sheets you can create to help students practice beginning-handwriting skills. After creating one of the practice pages suggested below, make a copy for each child and have him complete it as directed.

- Draw dotted lines, circles, curves, and zigzags. Have each child trace the lines.
- Draw several simple roads. Have each student draw a line down the middle of each road.
- Draw letters with missing parts. Have each child finish the letters.
- Draw a wagon wheel. Have each student draw the spokes.
- Draw balloons. Have each child draw a string for each balloon.

X Marks the Object

This listen-and-do activity makes practicing the letter *X* very easy.

1. Create a sheet with 12 different pictures on it. (If desired, use selected picture cards from pages 220–224.)
2. Make a copy for each child.
3. Give each student a copy of the sheet and a pencil.
4. Say the name of one of the objects and have each child use his pencil to write an *X* on it.

Writing Tickets

Wanted: good behavior! This student officer practices writing names while rewarding his classmates for kind behavior!

1. To prepare, make kindness tickets by dividing a sheet of paper into four sections.
2. At the top of each section, write "Kindness Ticket" and add a name line.
3. List some kind acts, such as helping a friend, playing quietly, and sharing.
4. Draw a box to the right of each kind act on the list.
5. Make several copies of the sheet and then cut them into fourths.
6. To make each ticket book, staple ten tickets together.
7. Each day invite a different child to be the kindness officer. Give the appointed officer a ticket book.
8. Have him issue tickets for kind behavior by writing the ticketed student's name on the line and then drawing a small smiley face in the box next to the appropriate kind deed. Then he tears the ticket out to give to the student he observed.

Order Pads

These pads make great writing practice for children who play restaurant. Order up!

1. Make several menus listing items and picture clues, such as a hamburger, a hot dog, a juice box, chips, a cookie, and a salad.
2. Laminate the menus for durability.
3. Make several order forms by dividing a sheet of paper into four sections.
4. Label the top of each section "Children's Cafe" and add writing lines if desired.
5. Make several copies of the sheet and then cut them into fourths.
6. Staple ten forms together to make an order pad.
7. Invite youngsters to act as servers and write orders on the forms while playing restaurant.

All-Occasion Cards

Everyone loves to receive a card, especially when it's written and decorated by a little one!

1. Fold construction paper sheets in half to create the cards.
2. Print traceable greetings inside the cards, such as "Happy Birthday," "Thank You," "Congratulations," and "Happy Holidays."
3. As a special occasion nears, have each child choose a card, decorate the front of it, and trace the message inside.
4. Instruct him to sign his name under the greeting and then give the card to its deserving recipient.

I Love You Cards

Love is in the air when your students write and share these thoughtful cards.

1. Give each child a sheet of construction paper.
2. Have her fold her paper in half.
3. Instruct her to unfold her paper and label the inside of the card as shown. Discuss the meaning of the heart with her.
4. Have her decorate the front of her card with markers, stickers, and other craft items.
5. Instruct each child to sign her name under her greeting before giving the card to a friend or loved one.

Congratulations Posters

Look for opportunities in your school or school community to congratulate people (such as when someone gets married, has a baby, retires, or wins an award), and you'll find inspiration for name-writing practice.

1. Set out a large piece of bulletin board paper and write "Congratulations!" in large letters on the paper.
2. Have each child take a turn signing his name on the paper, drawing a small picture, or writing a message.
3. When everyone has had a turn, roll up the paper, tie it with a large ribbon, and have your class (or a few student delegates) present it to the person you are congratulating.

"Wow" Cards

This fun idea not only inspires writing, but also inspires pride in each child who receives a card!

1. Write short, inspirational words on individual index cards and place them in your writing center.
2. Add blank index cards and some markers and stickers to the center too.
3. As a student visits the center, she chooses a word card and copies the word onto a blank card.
4. She decorates the card as desired.
5. Encourage each child to reward classmates with the cards she makes. Everyone will feel special!

TEC61200

TEC61200

TEC61200

TEC61200

162

✳ Letters and Sounds ✳

When guided in developmentally appropriate ways, young children benefit from learning to name alphabet letters, separate sounds in spoken words, and associate some sounds with the letters that represent them. These abilities are essential keys to reading and writing. Teachers can give children these keys by involving them in a wide range of playful experiences involving letters and sounds. That's where this section comes in. You'll find ideas for teaching letter knowledge, phonemic awareness, and phonics.

Getting to Know Letters

Centers

This section consists of ideas for integrating letter formation, letter names, and letter matching into:

- literacy centers
- book nook
- housekeeping area
- cooking corner
- block area
- art center
- outdoor play

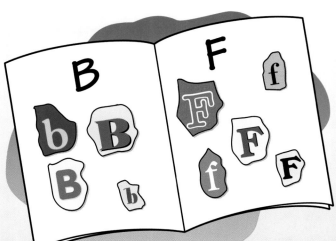

Literacy Centers

Letter Books

Students will be eager to work at this ongoing center!

Materials
plain paper
stapler
markers
letters cut from magazines and newspapers
glue sticks

Preparation
To make a booklet for each child, fold four sheets of paper in half and staple along the fold. Then have each child indicate seven letters she would like to explore. Label the front cover of the booklet with her name or have her do it. Then write each of the seven specified letters at the top of a booklet page. Place the booklets in a center with glue sticks and letters cut from magazines and newspapers.

Activity
Over several weeks, encourage each child to routinely visit the center, find her booklet, and choose a letter to focus on during center time. Then have her find and glue on letters that match the one written on that page. When the booklets are completed, encourage children to read them to their classmates and people at home.

Letter Boxes

Students play postal workers in this letter-sorting activity.

Materials
5 lidded shoeboxes
4 small index cards, each labeled with
  a different letter
small envelopes, each programmed with
  one of the letters on the cards
date stamp or stamp with a postal
  message such as "First Class" (optional)
stamp pad (optional)

Preparation
If desired, paint or cover each shoebox. Cut mail slots in the lids of four boxes, and attach a labeled index card to the end of each box. Set out another box nearby filled with labeled envelopes. If you want to have children stamp the mail as they sort it, provide a stamp and stamp pad.

Activity
Introduce this sorting activity to your students before including it at your literacy center. Show the children how to take turns sorting the mail by letter and stamping it. If several childen visit this center at once, have them name the letters as they drop them in the boxes.

Literacy Centers

Greetings

Modify this center to fit any season.

Materials
12 cutouts appropriate for   markers
   the season or holiday   small basket
12 envelopes

Preparation
Label the cutouts with an appropriate number of different letters, depending on which letters your children have been learning. Add seasonal greetings, if desired. Label an envelope to match each cutout. You may program these to be identical matches or uppercase and lowercase matches. Place the cutouts and the envelopes in a basket at the center.

Activity
Show children how to match cutouts with envelopes while referring to the letters. For those children who visit the center in pairs, have them tell their partners the name of each matched letter.

Letter Searches

Environmental print adds a special component to this center.

Materials
several newspaper and magazine   paper cup
   ads with large lettering   scissors
lamination materials   wipe-off markers
letters written on index cards   paper towels

Preparation
Laminate several ads and place them at a center with wipe-off markers. Invert a cup and cut a slit in the bottom. Insert a letter card in the slit. Place the cup and paper towels at the center.

Activity
Have children who visit the center observe the letter card and look for that letter on the laminated sheets. Each time the letter is discovered, have the child circle it. Before he erases his work and leaves the center, have him discuss the letter he circled with someone.

Card Matchup

This simple center requires little preparation but offers lots of learning opportunities.

Materials
deck of cards
resealable bag or envelope

Preparation
Collect the aces, jacks, queens, and kings from a deck of cards. Place these cards in a resealable bag or envelope.

Activity
Have children take turns sorting the *A*s, *K*s, *Q*s, and *J*s.

Letter Magnets

Watch word formation skills grow at this center.

Materials
uppercase alphabet magnets   cookie sheets (optional)
lowercase alphabet magnets   word cards or name cards

Preparation
Choose a location for this center near a surface that your magnets will stick to, such as a filing cabinet or metal room divider (or put cookie sheets in your center).

Activity
During circle time, give each child a word or name card; then show them how to form different words by using the magnets and referring to the cards. Ask each child to form his word for a classmate and, once he has finished it, to name the word.

At other times of the year, suggest that children visit this center and use the magnets to write their names, search for particular letters, or match uppercase and lowercase letters on the metal surface.

Literacy Centers

Letter Wheel

Learning letters using this letter wheel is a special treat for your little ones.

Materials
paper plate
markers
clothespins

Preparation
Use a marker to divide the plate into eight sections; then write an uppercase letter near the rim of each section. Label each of eight clothespins with a lowercase letter to match the letter on a section of the plate. (If desired, you may color-code the backs of the clothespins and the back of the plate for self-checking.)

Activity
Show students how to find a lowercase match for an uppercase letter on the plate and clip on the matching clothespin. Then encourage students to visit the literacy center to complete this activity.

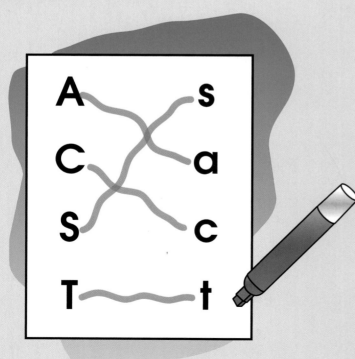

Letter Matchups

Matching letters is fun when students get to use a marker to show off their skills.

Materials
paper   wipe-off markers
marker   paper towels
laminating supplies

Preparation
Write four uppercase letters down the left side of a page and four corresponding lowercase letters in random order down the right side. Use die-cut letters for a colorful alternative. Laminate this page and others like it. Place them in the literacy center along with wipe-off markers and paper towels.

Activity
Discuss with students how to draw lines to match uppercase and lowercase letters on the page. Explain how they can confirm their answers using displays on your classroom walls and then clean the page for the next child's use.

Newspaper Search

Highlighters help students focus their attention on featured letters in this newsprint idea.

Materials
pages from a newspaper
construction paper letter cutouts

glue
highlighters

Preparation
Glue a letter cutout near the top of each newspaper page. Attach these pages to a wall in your center and put a few highlighters nearby.

Activity
As children visit this center, have them name the large colorful letter on the newspaper. Then have them find that letter elsewhere on the newspaper page and highlight it each time they find it.

Nailing Letters

This tactile center will draw students in again and again.

Materials
permanent marker
8" foam squares
basket

golf tees
resealable plastic bag
toy hammer

Preparation
Use the marker to write a large letter on each foam square. Store the squares in a basket along with a bag of golf tees and the hammer.

Activity
Introduce this activity to reinforce the formation of the letters your children are learning. Show children how to use the hammer to nail tees into each space along the lines of a foam letter. After each child completely covers his letter with tees, have him share his square with other children and tell them about the letter and its form. Have each child remove the tees from the foam he used and return them to the bag before leaving the center.

Book Nook
Letter Pillows

These cozy letters invite students to expand their letter recognition skills.

Materials
giant uppercase letter patterns (your choice of letters)
marker
large pieces of felt
scissors
needle
thread
fiberfill

Preparation
Have an adult volunteer trace each letter pattern onto a double thickness of felt and then cut out each letter, cutting through both thicknesses. Then have her stitch around the edge through both thicknesses, leaving a couple of different openings in the stitching. Have her finish each letter by stuffing it with fiberfill and sewing the openings closed. Place the pillows in the reading area.

Activity
When a child chooses a pillow to rest on, ask her what letter she has chosen. Then encourage her to look for that letter in the book that she's reading.

Letter Glasses

This clever idea will open students' eyes to a new way of looking for letters.

Materials
several pairs of children's plastic sunglasses
permanent markers
eyeglass cases

Preparation
Program the frames of a pair of sunglasses with a letter that children are learning, and program an eyeglass case to match. Similarly, program several sunglass/case sets with different letters. If the lenses are very dark, you may want to remove them so that wearing them will not hamper reading. Store these letter glasses in their cases near your classroom book display.

Activity
Introduce these glasses and their use during circle time one day. Explain that children are invited to wear a pair of these glasses when they visit the book corner. As each child wears the glasses, have him keep the case nearby so that he can frequently refer to the letter on it. Then, as he is reading, ask him to be in search of the letter on his case.

Book Nook

Letter Basket

This special display shelf or basket features a single letter and books that have extra emphasis on that letter.

Materials
index card · literature books related
marker · to the chosen letter
tape · basket or shelf

Preparation
Determine a letter you'd like to feature, and write it on an index card. Attach the card to a shelf or basket in your reading area. Select literature that highlights the letter, and place it on the shelf or in the basket.

Activity
Remind students of the special letter featured in your reading area. Encourage visitors to name the letter on the card. Then have them watch for that letter as they enjoy the specially selected stories.

Book Wraps

These special wraps mark books that feature a special letter and definitely catch your students' attention!

Materials
18" x 2" strips of · literature books
construction paper · related to the
markers · chosen letter
tape · stickers (optional)

Preparation
Determine a letter you'd like to feature, and write it near the middle of several strips of paper. Decorate the strips with stickers if desired. Wrap the strips, as shown, around the covers of several books that feature the letter. Tape the strip inside the cover where the ends overlap. (Hint: Keep the tape only on the strip to prevent damage to the book.)

Activity
When a student selects a book with a letter wrap, ask him to name the letter for his classmates in the center and then read the book with an eye toward the special letter.

Housekeeping Area

Letter Dress-Up Clothes

Alphabet-print fabric dresses up your housekeeping area and encourages letter practice.

Materials
alphabet-print fabric
thread

Preparation
Have adult volunteers use the fabric to make a variety of items for your housekeeping area. With a few scissor snips, rectangles of this fabric can quickly become capes, baby blankets, or tablecloths. Suggest that experienced seamstresses make aprons, vests, pillows, or curtains for the housekeeping area.

Activity
Encourage students to use the alphabet fabric as they engage in imaginative role-playing. Then, when little ones are playing, prompt them to recognize and name specific letters. Hey, that's the letter *G!*

Letter Clothesline

You'll hang on to this creative way to introduce letter practice into your housekeeping area.

Materials
8" squares of solid-
   colored fabric
markers
string

2 chairs
clothespins
laundry basket

Preparation
Write a large letter on each of the fabric squares. Place them in a laundry basket near a clothesline made from two chairs and string. Put the clothespins nearby.

Activity
Ask pairs of children to play at the clothesline together. Have them take turns hanging up the fabric squares. Before a child clips up a square, have him determine the letter name with the help of his partner. If they are unsure about the letter name, have them ask an adult for help. Before leaving the center, have the children take turns removing squares from the line and saying the letter names as they drop the squares back into the laundry basket.

Letter Boxes

Stock your houskeeping center cupboards with these letter boxes, and watch kids' letter skills stack up!

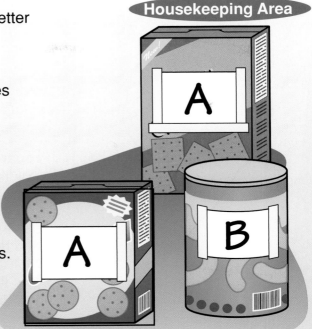

Housekeeping Area

Materials
assortment of empty cardboard food containers and boxes
construction paper
glue or tape
markers
large baskets or tote bags (optional, for shopping)

Preparation
Mask the text on each box (or cover the whole box) with construction paper. Then write a letter on each box, making sure that several containers have matching letters. Place the boxes on shelves or in cupboards in your housekeeping area. Place baskets or tote bags nearby if desired.

Activity
Have students visit the center and shop or search for containers with matching letters. If desired, have a student put her matching items in a tote bag or basket. Encourage each child to name the letter she shopped for and to say its sound if possible.

Letter Hats

Top off some housekeeping play with an activity that puts hats to new use.

Materials
assorted hats   tape
index cards   markers

Preparation
Make a letter label for each hat by writing a letter on an index card and attaching it to the hat. You can limit the letters to a small set your students are studying, or you can coordinate the letter with the type of hat, such as *N* for a nurse's hat or *F* for a firefighter's hat. Add the hats to your housekeeping center.

Activity
As youngsters play with the hats, encourage them to name the letters and incorporate them into their play. (For example, a child wearing a chef's hat might be called "Cook *C*" or the youngster in the nurse hat might be named "Nurse *N*.")

Cooking Corner

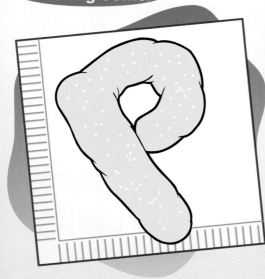

Dough Letters

These edible letters make learning tasty.

Materials

marker
foil
aprons
refrigerated biscuit dough
cookie sheet

flour
salt or cinnamon-sugar mixture
butter (melted)
pastry brush
napkins

Preparation

Write each child's name on a square of foil. Place the squares on a tabletop and sprinkle a little flour on each one.

Activity

As each child dons an apron and takes a turn visiting the cooking corner, have him roll an uncooked refrigerated biscuit into a long, snakelike form. Then have him choose a letter and find the letter on display in the classroom. Discuss the shape of the letter before having him form his dough into a matching shape. Help each child place his letter on his foil square and then place his square on a cookie sheet. Brush on melted butter, add salt or cinnamon sugar, and then bake the letters in a preheated oven at 350° until they are well browned. Serve them for a yummy snack with lots of conversation about letters.

Frosting Letters

Letter formation turns into a real treat when it's done with frosting.

Materials

white frosting
food coloring (optional)
paper

crayons
graham crackers or large sugar cookies
plastic knives or new craft sticks

Preparation

To tie in seasonal themes, tint white frosting with food coloring before children arrive at the center. Place the frosting, paper, crayons, crackers or cookies, and utensils nearby.

Activity

Give each visitor at the cooking corner a cookie or cracker. Have him choose a letter and describe its form. To practice making the letter, have him write it in crayon on a sheet of paper. Then have him use a plastic knife or craft stick to write the letter in frosting on the cookie or cracker. Provide assistance as necessary and then help each child put his creation away until snacktime. Before these treats get devoured, ask children to tell their classmates about their letters.

Letter Pretzels

Students will love nibbling pretzels into letter shapes.

Materials
bag of pretzel twists   bowls
bag of pretzel sticks   napkins

Preparation
Set out the pretzels in bowls and place a napkin at each seat.

Activity
As each child visits the cooking corner, let her experiment with pretzel letter formation by chewing off parts of a couple of pretzel twists to make letter parts. Then have her use stick pretzels and/or pretzel parts to form letters. When a child has formed one letter, encourage her to rearrange her pieces to make another letter. How many letters can she make before giving in and gobbling down her pretzels?

Celery Letters

Celery is the basis for this letter formation fun.

Materials
celery stalks sliced widthwise into C shapes
napkins

Preparation
Place a few slices of celery on a napkin for each visitor at the cooking corner.

Activity
Encourage each child to move the celery slices around on his napkin. Encourage him to arrange them to resemble *c*'s, *o*'s, and *s*'s. Can he make other letters from them before he eats them for a snack?

Block Area

Block Letters

Build literacy skills by having students build letters in your block area.

Materials
wooden blocks
large uppercase letter cutout or masking tape
camera (optional)

Preparation
Put a large uppercase letter on the wall in the block center or make a tape outline on the carpet in the center.

Activity
Encourage your children to make the featured letter from blocks in the block area. If desired, photograph each letter made (either with its crafters or children whose names begin with that letter) and put the photos into an album. Place the album in the reading area and encourage children to read it and talk about the letters.

Blocks

Alphabet Block Match

Try this twist on using traditional alphabet blocks.

Materials
alphabet blocks
letter cards that match the letters on the blocks

Preparation
Introduce and demonstrate this matching activity at circle time and encourage children to try it when visiting the block area. In the beginning, include only three or four cards in the center. Add to the deck as children's abilities advance.

Activity
Have children take turns choosing a card and finding the blocks with matching letters.

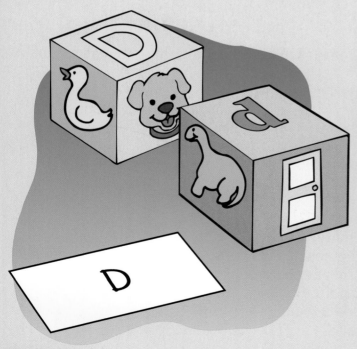

Block Area

Storage Letters

Even center cleanup or setup can be educational with this quick idea.

Materials
index cards
marker
tape

Preparation
Label several index cards with letters your children are learning. Tape the letters to bins or shelves in the block area to represent different storage areas.

Activity
When you ask a child to get some blocks or to put them away, refer to the area you would like them to go to by saying the name of the letter.

Letter Cars

Vroom! There's no stopping the fast-paced learning taking place at this center.

Materials
toy cars, buses, and trucks
masking tape
marker

Preparation
Using masking tape and a marker, label each of the vehicles in your block area with a letter your children have been discussing.

Activity
Have each child choose a car by naming the letter on it. Then ask children to use blocks to form a raceway. Supervise race events and discuss each race afterward with children, referring to the cars by letter.

Or, if your labels include uppercase and lowercase matches, encourage each driver to drive around the block area to find the vehicle with the letter that matches his.

Street Signs

These creative signs put letters in your students' paths during playtime.

Materials
permanent marker
green poster board rectangles
clear Con-Tact covering
scissors
yardsticks
coffee cans or buckets
gravel or sand
nail polish remover (optional)

Preparation
Place two rectangles on a piece of clear Con-Tact covering (sticky side up) so that when the covering is folded, the rectangles are back to back. Fold the covering and trim around the sign as needed. Label each side with a letter children are learning. Unseal the bottom edge to insert a yardstick. Fill each coffee can about two-thirds full with gravel or sand, and then push a yardstick sign into the gravel or sand. Place several street signs around the area where children ride wheeled toys.

To change the signs to other letters, remove each letter using nail polish remover and then reprogram.

Activity
Encourage children to use the street names during outdoor play conversations.

Sidewalk Letters

A sunny sidewalk is the perfect backdrop for this letter practice.

Materials
nametags
sidewalk chalk
sidewalk or paved area

Activity
On a sunny day, find a place outside where your children can write on a sidewalk or paved area. Have children take their nametags outside with them. Give each child some thick colored chalk and encourage him to make the first letter in his name or the first letters in the names of his classmates. Afterward, ask for volunteers to read and talk about the letters that they wrote.

Outdoor Play

mud

Sand and Dirt Letters

Dirt and water are the perfect formula for practicing letter writing!

Materials
wooden dowels
sand or dirt
water (optional)

poster board squares
marker

Preparation
Prepare the sand or dirt for writing by smoothing it. Add some water to it, if desired. Fold poster board squares in half so that they are self-standing. Place a few around the sand or mud area.

Activity
Explain to children that they may use the dowels to write in the sand or mud. Ask them if they would like you to write any letters or spell any words for them, and write their suggested letters and words on the poster boards. Add a few words like "mud" to the list, if desired. Encourage children to use the cards as a guide while they write in the wet sand or mud.

Outdoor Markings

Labels turn play into letter practice.

Materials
letter stickers or adhesive vinyl letters

Preparation
Use the letters to label areas of your playground or pieces of equipment.

Activity
When talking to children about options for play, refer to the objects by the names of the letters on them. Then confirm that children understand the equipment or area that you're suggesting by having them point to the letter you've indicated.

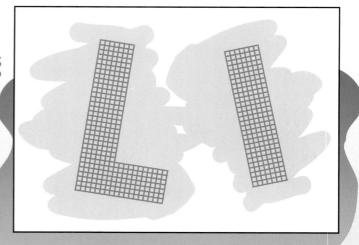

Art Center

Bumpy Lettering

Textures add to the fun of learning letters at this art center.

Materials
tagboard squares
pencil
glue
scissors
plastic canvas
    and/or sandpaper

masking tape
plain paper
crayons (wrappers
    removed)

Preparation
Write a large letter on each piece of tagboard. Then snip the cap of a glue bottle to make the opening larger than normal. Squirt a thick line of glue over each letter, and set the tagboard aside to dry for about 48 hours. Then tape the squares to a tabletop in your writing center and place plain paper and crayons nearby. Later in the year, make similar textured letters for rubbings by cutting letters from plastic canvas and/or sandpaper. Children will love the different textures.

Activity
Have children who visit the center choose a letter, put paper on top of it, and rub it with the side of a crayon to reveal the letter form beneath.

Play Dough Letters

Play dough adds punch to this simple activity.

Materials
vinyl tablecloth or bulletin board paper
markers
play dough

Preparation
Spread a vinyl tablecloth or bulletin board paper over a table in your art area. Then use markers to write letters on the tablecloth or paper to represent the letters your children have been learning. Put play dough in containers on the table.

Activity
Invite children to visit this center, roll the dough into long snakelike forms, and use the forms to cover the lines of several letters. Before they put their dough away, have them tell classmates about the letters they made.

Waxy Letters · Art Center

Letter formation has never been so fun!

Materials
Wikki Stix creatables
wooden or plastic letters or a tablecloth with letters
   written on it

Preparation
During circle time, show students how Wikki Stix
creatables can be bent into the shapes of letters. Then
place the Wikki Stix creatables in your art center along with
letters for models or a tablecloth with letters written on it.

Activity
Have each child visit the center and make a letter or
two, referring to the models provided as necessary.

Sponge Letters

Paint is a favorite of youngsters, and you'll
appreciate the letter practice that goes with it!

Materials
three 3" sponge letters
3 plastic juice cans, empty
hot glue gun or craft glue
3 colors of tempera paint
3 shallow disposable containers

paper towels
smocks
art paper
easel

Preparation
Glue a letter-shaped sponge to the bottom of each empty plastic juice can
after verifying that the letter will be oriented correctly when printed. (These
juice-can handles are easy for preschoolers to hold, can decrease the
amount of paint that gets on children's hands, and improve the impressions
made by the letter sponges.) Line the shallow containers with several
thicknesses of paper towels; then pour a different color of tempera paint into
each container. Put a letter can by each color of paint.

Activity
During circle time, introduce this art activity to your children. Demonstrate
how to choose a letter and, holding on to the can, press the letter first into
the paint and then onto art paper attached to an easel. Explain that more
than one print can be made before the sponge needs to be reloaded with
paint, and encourage children to say the letter name each time they make a
print. Children may use just one letter or all of them!

Art Center

Crayon Resist Letters

Crayon and paint team up to reveal a special surprise!

Materials
white crayon
white art paper

thinned tempera paint
wide brushes

Preparation
Use a white crayon to write a single letter per page on a class supply of white art paper. Place the paper at the art center along with wide brushes and tempera paint thinned almost to the consistency of watercolor.

Activity
Have each child take a turn at this center, painting the entire page to reveal the secret letter. Encourage children to discuss the letters that appear while they paint. When the paintings have dried, find out who can name her letter and who has a letter that matches someone else's letter.

Letter Collage

All shapes and sizes of letters are welcome on these creative collages.

Materials
letters of all colors and sizes cut from ads
glue sticks
8" tagboard squares

Preparation
If desired, have children locate and cut out letters and add them to a box of letters that will later be used for this collage. When a large collection of letters is available, place glue sticks and tagboard squares in the art center.

Activity
Introduce this activity during circle time. Show children a collage that you have started, and demonstrate how letters are added to it. Explain that lots and lots of letters can be used on a collage. After each child has worked on a collage, have him tell a partner about some of the letters his artwork contains.

Art Center

Decorating Letters

Feature a specific letter using this art activity.

Materials
large outlined letter for each child
glue sticks
photocopied letters

Preparation
On various colors of paper, photocopy the same letter in a variety of fonts, sizes, and uppercase and lowercase forms. Cut out these letters and place them in the art center along with glue sticks.

Activity
Demonstrate this art activity during center time. Talk about the featured letter and all the different forms it takes. Then show students how to glue the letters inside the outline of the large letter. Explain that they can create these colorful letters when they visit the art center. If desired, after each child has visited the center, help him cut the letter out. Encourage lots of conversation at home and at school about this featured letter.

Letter Stamps

The fun just goes on and on at this center filled with letter stamps.

Materials
letter stamps, preferably with handles
art paper
stamp pads
damp paper towels

Preparation
Set out some letter stamps, stamp pads, and art paper. Also place a stack of damp paper towels in the center for cleaning the stamps.

Activity
Show your children how to press a stamp onto a stamp pad and then onto their papers. Ask them to say the letter name whenever they stamp one and to stamp lots and lots of letters. Then give a demonstration on how to clean the stamps.

Art Center

Fingerpainting

"Look what I made!" will be echoing from your art center when students take part in this fingerpainting project.

Materials
fingerpaint
fingerpainting paper
spray bottle containing water
cutouts of letters

Preparation
Place cutouts of familiar letters on the wall near the art area.

Activity
For each child at the center, mist a sheet of paper with water and drop on a dollop of fingerpaint. Encourage free-form artistic exploration. Then ask each child to look at a letter on the wall and use his finger to write that letter in the fingerpaint. Gauge how many letters children should write by their levels of interest. Remist the papers as necessary. Later, when the paintings are dry, have the creators of the masterpieces tell about the letters they wrote.

Cookie Cutter Prints

See what these cookie cutters add to this printing activity.

Materials
letter-shaped cookie cutters   paper towels
tempera paint   art paper
shallow containers

Preparation
Set out the art paper and letter-shaped cookie cutters. Line one or more shallow containers with several thicknesses of paper towels; then pour tempera paint onto the paper towels.

Activity
Show children how to choose a cookie cutter letter, name it, and then dip it into the paint. Next, show them how to press the cutter onto paper to make an impression of the letter. Encourage children to make as many letter impressions as they wish on their papers. When the paintings are dry, staple them to make a class booklet. Share the booklet at circle time and have each child tell about at least one letter on his page.

Getting to Know Letters

✳ •••• Group Time •••• ✳

This section includes large- and small-group activities to promote:

- letter formation
- letter recognition
- letter naming

Beginning Letter Pals

It's fun to discover that your name shares its beginning letter with the name of a class-mate or maybe even a cartoon character.

1. In advance, prepare a nametag for each child.
2. Consider which children have class-mates whose names begin with the same letter. If there isn't a classmate with a matching initial letter, locate a picture of a cartoon character or other recognizable personality whose name's initial letter is a match. Prior to the activity, post these pictures with nametags near your circle-time area.
3. To begin, have each child bring her nametag to circle time.
4. As children look at their names, discuss the first letters.
5. Have them walk around looking for classmates holding nametags that begin with the same first letters as theirs do. If a child doesn't find a match among her classmates, have her check out the cartoon characters to find a match.
6. Return to the circle and have children discuss the matches and the letter names.

Raise Your Hand for Letters

This easy activity will have your children scanning their names in hopes of making a letter match.

1. Give each child a nametag.
2. Hold up an alphabet card, say the name of the letter, and have a child describe the shape of it.
3. Ask children to look for that letter on their nametags. If they find it, have them raise their hands or stand up. Call on children to show their classmates the matching letters in their names.
4. Repeat this activity several times, having children search for a variety of letters.

Fishing for Letters

A fun way to learn letter names is to take your children fishing!

1. Make a simple fishing game with 16 paper fish shapes, paper clips, a wooden spoon or dowel, and a magnet on a string.
2. Program four of the fish shapes for each of four letters you wish to feature, and then attach a paper clip to the mouth area of each.
3. Tie the string to the spoon or dowel and place the fish on the floor. Time to fish!
4. To play, have your children take turns fishing.
5. When a child catches a fish, ask him to name the letter. Provide assistance as needed.
6. Have him put the fish back with the others before the next player takes his turn.
7. Continue in this manner until interest fades.

Letter Stones

Little learners will step gingerly across this rushing river—if they can name some letters.

1. Place five or more labeled stone cutouts to create a path across an imaginary river. Tape them in place.
2. Have your children stand at one end of the line of stones and explain that there is a river in front of them and these stones create a path for crossing it.
3. Tell children that when a child jumps on a letter, she must name it in order to keep going. If she has trouble remembering the letter name, she may go to the end of the line, where she will have time to hear others name all the letters before her next turn.
4. Have each child cross the river. Provide assistance when needed.

Letter Tickets

Take an imaginary bus out for a spin to reinforce letter identification.

1. Create a bus by lining up two rows of chairs. Place a driver's chair at the front.
2. Make a letter card for each seat on your bus, and make a duplicate set of letter cards to use as bus tickets.
3. Tape the seat cards to the seat backs.
4. Give each child a letter-card ticket. Have him board the bus to find a matching letter on a seat back and then sit in that seat.
5. When everyone is seated, have each child turn and put his ticket beside his seat letter to double-check the match and say the letter name. Then collect the tickets.
6. Take your seat in the driver's seat and pretend to drive along as you and your children sing an alphabet song or "The Wheels on the Bus."
7. Unload the bus and repeat the activity, giving children different letters to find and identify.

Letter Corners

This variation on the traditional Four Corners game will have your children scampering from one letter recognition opportunity to another.

1. Tape one of four different letter cards in each corner of your room.
2. Write the same four letters on four small cards and put them in a bag.
3. Have each child choose a corner to stand in, observe its letter, and discuss the letter name with his classmates.
4. Draw one of the letter cards from the bag and call out the letter (or have a child do it). Have each child who's standing in the corner labeled with that letter sit down near the center of the room. Return the card to the bag.
5. The remaining children standing continue the game by choosing which corner to stand in for the next round, observing its letter, and determining its letter name.
6. Continue in this fashion until there is one child standing.

Go Fish

In this fishy card game for four players, the catch of the day is letter recognition.

1. Remove the aces, kings, queens, and jacks from four card decks and shuffle these cards.
2. Deal five cards to each player; then place the deck facedown in the middle of the table.
3. Have each player check his cards for letter pairs that match, such as two *J*s. Any player who has matching pairs places each pair faceup in front of him.
4. Have the first player ask any other player for a letter to match any of the ones he already has. If the player has the requested card, he gives it to the first player, who places the match on the tabletop in front of him.
5. Have the first player repeat this until the person he requests a card from does not have the requested letter and says, "Go fish." The first player then takes the top card from the deck. If it matches one of his other cards, he lays the pair down; if not, he holds the card.
6. Have the other players take their turns in the same way.
7. The game continues until either the deck or a player runs out of cards. The winner is the player who has the most pairs of letters.

Letter Feely Bag

Here's an easy way to put a tactile spin on letter identification.

1. Put some small plastic or wooden letters in a cloth bag.
2. Have a child reach into the bag and hold one letter, feeling its shape.
3. Ask her to talk about the shape of the letter and identify it before removing it from the bag to confirm its identity. If she does not correctly name the letter on the first try, have her put it back in the bag. If she does correctly name it, have her put the letter in front of her.
4. Repeat this process as each child takes a turn.
5. At the end of the game, ask children who have letters to tell what their letters are before returning them to the bag.

Flashlight Letters

Bring a little of nighttime's mystery into your school day with this letter recognition activity.

1. Obtain a flashlight. Then darken the class-room and have your children gather in front of a blank wall.
2. Using the flashlight as a pencil, write a large letter form on the wall. Describe how you're forming the letter as you make it.
3. Ask children to guess which letter you wrote. Provide assistance as necessary.
4. Repeat, featuring several other letters.

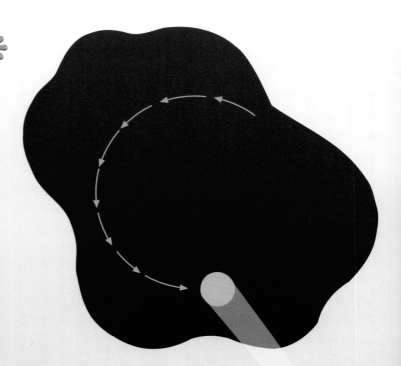

Back Letters

This is an all-time favorite with young children. Through the sense of touch, this activity helps your children visualize how letters are written.

1. Using your finger, write a large letter on a child's back.
2. Ask him to identify the letter you wrote. If he needs help, write it on his back again or write it on the board.
3. Repeat this several times with different children.
4. When everyone understands how the game is played, encourage your children to play it with each other or with an adult at home.

Letter Necklaces

This activity lets your children create their own necklaces and improve their letter recognition at the same time.

1. For each child, provide a 1" x 24" strip of tissue paper, markers, and a four-inch poster board circle with two holes punched side by side. Set out the circles along with some markers.
2. Have each child choose a letter from among the letters you've recently talked about for you to write on her circle.
3. Have her use markers to decorate it.
4. Help each child fold and thread her tissue paper strip through her letter circle and tie the ends of the strip.
5. Have each child model her necklace for her classmates and tell the name of the letter and something about its form.

Letter Concentration

This traditional memory game for two players makes letter matching and identification a whole lot of fun.

1. Start with eight letter cards featuring only four different letters (two cards for each letter). As children's skills build and they become familiar with the game, more letter cards can be added.
2. Place the cards facedown randomly on a tabletop.
3. Have two players each take turns turning over a pair of cards in an effort to find a letter match. If the letters match, the child puts the cards by him. If the letters do not match, the child returns them to their original positions.
4. Play continues until all the cards have been paired.

Letter Lotto

Challenge your children's listening and letter recognition skills with this ever-popular game.

1. Prepare a nine-inch square tagboard gameboard for each player. Use a marker to divide each gameboard into nine three-inch squares.
2. On each of 12 index cards write a different letter.
3. Label each gameboard with nine of the 12 letters on your index cards. Rotate the locations of the letters on the gameboards so that no two gameboards are alike.
4. Provide each player with a gameboard and nine three-inch construction paper squares to use as game markers.
5. Draw an index card from the facedown deck and call out the letter. Have each player cover that letter if it appears on his board.
6. Play continues in this manner until a player covers the entire board. She says, "Lotto!" to signal her win.
7. Confirm her answers and play again!

Body Letters

If you're a shutterbug (or if one of your children's parents is), this activity is going to result in letter recognition fun that will last the whole year through.

1. Show your children how they can make some letters with their bodies. Have them curl up into *C*s and *J*s or stretch out into *T*s *Y*s and *K*s. Take at least one photo for each different letter formed.
2. Have your children find partners and try making *A*s, *D*s, and *H*s. Snap some photos.
3. Have groups of children try making *W*s, *B*s, and *E*s and then take more photos.
4. Determine which letters of the alphabet remain unphotographed and have volunteers pose for those photos.
5. Put the photos in alphabetical order in an album and have children read their way through the album, saying each letter name.

Beginning Sounds

This section includes ideas that provide practice with the following:

- **individual sounds**

- **matching sounds**

- **identifying the beginning sounds of words**

- **identifying words that begin with different sounds**

Food Cards

All your little ones will have a big appetite for this easy beginning-sound sorting task.

1. Cut from magazines four pictures of foods that start with each of these letters: *B, S, T.* Glue the pictures to index cards.
2. Color-code the backs of the index cards so that each letter sound is represented by a different color.
3. Randomly put the cards on a tabletop with the pictures facing up.
4. Have children say the picture words, sort them by beginning sounds, and discuss how they grouped them.
5. Have children flip the cards over to confirm that the initial consonants match.

Car and can!

Same Sounds

Do these objects begin with the same sound or not? Children will be eager to listen to find out.

1. Gather several sets of three objects in which two objects share the same beginning sound.
2. At circle time, place one of the sets in front of you and ask the children to say the object names.
3. Have a child determine which two objects share the same beginning sound and explain how he knows.
4. Repeat this process with each of the other sets.

/B/, /B/, Bear!

Play this adaptation of Duck, Duck, Goose to practice beginning sounds.

1. Seat students in a circle and pick one child to be It.
2. Instead of saying "duck," the selected child chooses a letter (or uses the letter of the week) and says its sound as he touches each child's head.
3. When the child is ready to choose someone for the chase, he names a word that begins with that letter sound.
4. Play continues in this manner until everyone has had a turn.

Action Sounds

Children can generate words with the same beginning sounds as they dance, hop, and march the wiggles away.

1. Ask your children to run in place for just a few seconds. Then say, "Freeze!"
2. While children are catching their breath, ask whether anyone can say the sound at the beginning of the word *run*.
3. Then ask them to think of other words that begin with the /r/ sound. Discuss their answers.
4. Continue the game in the same manner with other movements and their initial letters. For example, try marching for the /m/ sound, hopping for the /h/ sound, dancing for the /d/ sound, and bending for the /b/ sound.

Sound Safari

Hunting for items with a particular beginning sound is a captivating way to improve your children's phonemic awareness.

1. At circle time, tell children you are going on a safari today.
2. Show children an object, such as a book, and have them determine its beginning sound.
3. Explain that the first safari will be in search of words that begin with the /b/ sound. Then set out with your children to search your classroom for the items. If you have a recording that might be appropriate for a safari, play it during your search.
4. Each time students find something that starts with the /b/ sound, have them say the word over and over, emphasizing the beginning sound. If the object can be brought back to camp (circle time), bring it along for the rest of the safari.
5. Once back at camp, talk about the words with the /b/ sound that were discovered.

Sound Concentration

The challenge in this small-group game is listening for beginning sounds and remembering which cards are where.

1. Choose four initial sounds for this game. Find two pictures for each sound and glue them to index cards. (If desired, use selected picture cards from pages 220–224.)
2. Put the cards in two rows facedown on a tabletop.
3. Have your children take turns turning over two cards, saying the picture words, and listening to determine whether they begin with the same beginning sound. If a child finds a match, he may keep the cards. If not, he returns them to their original positions.
4. Play continues until all of the cards have been used.

Is There a /k/?

Focus your students' listening skills and build phonological awareness skills at the same time.

1. Place a photocopied photo of each child in a paper bag. Draw a photo out of the bag and show it to students.
2. Ask students to show a thumbs-up if a letter sound you say is heard at the beginning of the pictured child's name. For example, you might say, "Is there a /n/ in *Nicky*?"
3. After quizzing youngsters once or twice with different letter sounds, have the pictured child hold his photo.
4. When all photos have been distributed, instruct students to hold up their photos and show a thumbs-up if they hear you say a letter sound that can be heard at the beginning of their names.

Nursery Rhyme Sounds

Using nursery rhymes, it's easy to entice children to determine the initial sounds of words.

1. Tell your children that you are going to say some rhymes but you need their help. Pretend that you have forgotten the first sound in the last word in each line and that you'll need them to supply the beginning sound.
2. Start a rhyme. Say one line at a time, but omit the last word and wait for children to supply its beginning sound.
3. Blend the beginning sound children supply with the remainder of the word to complete the line.
4. Repeat this process with each line of the rhyme.

Jack and Jill went up the...

/h/

/h/ /il/
Jack and Jill went up the hill!

Puffs of P

Maybe your children won't blow houses down quite like the wolf did, but they may be surprised at the puff of air the /p/ sound makes.

1. Draw three houses on separate sheets of paper. You may want these to resemble the three pigs' houses from the traditional tale.
2. Give three children the papers and ask each child to think of a different word that begins with the /p/ sound. Verify their decisions.
3. As a class, say the rhyme at the right.
4. Then, in turn, have each of the three children hold his paper near his mouth and say the word he chose while his classmates notice that the puff the /p/ sound makes actually moves the paper.
5. Repeat the activity with different children playing the three special speaking parts.

Three little pigs went out to play,
Leaving their homes unguarded one day.
Along came a wolf who knew what to say
To get those houses to blow away.

paper

Fishing for /f/ sounds
What will I catch?
A fork, a feather, a fig?

Sometimes I catch
The silliest things,
And sometimes I catch a fish!

Fishing for Fs

Here's a fun game to play when learning the /f/ sound.

1. Draw or glue pictures of words that start with F on small index cards. (If desired, use selected picture cards from pages 220–224.) Include several silly fish cards plus a few picture words that don't start with F.
2. Put these cards in a bag or bucket.
3. Recite the rhyme (left), asking your children to join in.
4. Have three children take turns reaching into the container and fishing for a picture card. If a child draws a card with a picture that does not start with the /f/ sound, have him draw another one.
5. When three children have drawn F cards, say the rhyme again, inserting their F words in the place of those in the third line.

Wishing Well

If you've been wishing for a game to make the /w/ sound come alive, wish no more!

1. Have your children decorate a large box or basket to be your wishing well.
2. Then make some picture cards of objects whose names start with *W* and some that do not. (If desired, use selected picture cards from pages 220–224.)
3. To play the wishing well game, have a child draw a card, hold it up, and say the picture word.
4. Have him determine whether the object's name begins with the /w/ sound. If it does, have him throw it in the well. If it does not, set it aside.
5. Continue in this manner, having several children take turns.

Bag It!

Who knew a paper bag could inspire so much learning?

1. Give each youngster a paper lunch bag and her photocopied picture.
2. Have her glue the picture to the front of the bag. Then have her draw pictures of small items whose names begin with the same sound as her name.
3. Have each youngster take her bag home and (with parental permission) place in it one or two of the items she drew. Have each child return the bag to school the following day.
4. Invite each child to say her name and then share the items from her bag, stressing the initial sounds.
5. Divide students into small groups so that no two children's names begin with the same sound. Have each group pool their bag contents and then sort them into the correct bags by matching the beginning sound of each item with the appropriate child's name.

Sounds of Summer

This activity can be adapted for any season and any beginning sound. Let's do summer and /s/!

1. Make a beach-themed display using all kinds of beach items, including several that begin with the /s/ sound. For example, you might include sand, a sun, a sailboat, sunscreen, and a starfish.
2. Set out some small sticky notes with the letter *S* printed on them.
3. During transition times, have your children tag the objects on the display that start with the /s/ sound.
4. When many of the objects have stickies on them, discuss the labels and how children reached their decisions.
5. Remove the stickies. Invite children to find other beach-related pictures to add to the display, especially ones whose names start with the /s/ sound.
6. Repeat the activity as before.

Seasonal Pairs

Here's another seasonal twist to beginning sound practice.

1. Set up a seasonal display table with pairs of objects so that the items in a pair begin with the same letter. For a winter display, you might include a mug and mittens and a coat and a cap. Arrange the objects randomly so that the pairs are not obvious.
2. As your children visit the display, have them say the names of the objects and sort them into pairs by beginning sounds.
3. After most children have visited the display, discuss the matching pairs during circle time.
4. Change the display for more seasonal matching practice.

L Is for Locket

Lots of learning takes place when your little ones make these lovely locket necklaces.

1. To make a locket for each child, fold a 4½" x 6" piece of construction paper in half. Cut a three-inch circle from it so that a portion of the fold is left intact, making two connected circles. Unfold the paper and hole-punch the top of the circle on the right. Place a hole reinforcer over the hole. Then tie a 24-inch length of crepe streamer through the hole to make a necklace.

2. Provide each child with a locket, an old magazine, scissors, and glue. Instruct her to find and cut out pictures of items whose names begin with the /l/ sound and then glue them to the inside of the locket.

3. After the glue has dried, help each youngster attach the hook and loop sides of a small Velcro fastener to keep the locket closed.

4. Invite each child to share her lovely locket with classmates.

Sounds on a String!

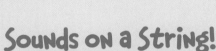

Here's a placemat game that reinforces phonemic awareness skills.

1. Find a placemat that has a simple design of different pictures, similar to the one shown. (If desired, use selected picture cards from the pages 220–224 to make a placemat.)

2. Pick six small objects. Each object's name should have the same beginning sound as that of a pictured item. Punch six holes around the edge of the placemat. Tie one end of a 12-inch yarn length to each hole. Hot-glue a different object to the loose end of each yarn length.

3. To play, a student matches each object to a picture on the placemat whose name begins with the same sound.

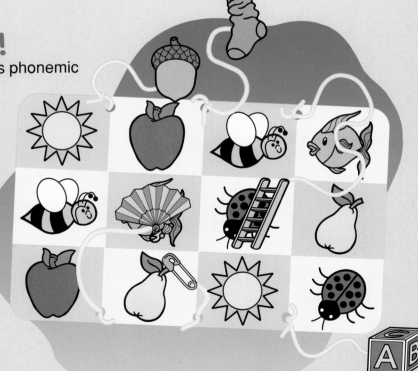

What's Missing?

Play this visual memory game and help your youngsters learn initial letter sounds.

1. Collect a variety of small items whose names begin with the same sound, such as a paper clip, pencil, pig, and pen for the /p/ sound. Then attach a small hook-side piece of a Velcro fastener to each object.
2. During group time, show each item to students and talk about its beginning sound; then place the objects on a flannelboard. After all the objects have been displayed, have each child close his eyes.
3. Remove one object and have youngsters open their eyes.
4. In turn, invite each child to guess which object was removed. Have the first child who guesses correctly tell you the sound the object's name begins with.
5. Repeat the activity, but this time have the child who gave the correct answer remove the object from the flannelboard.

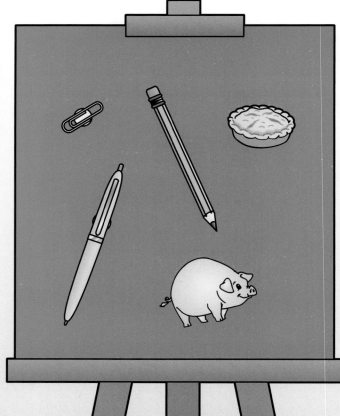

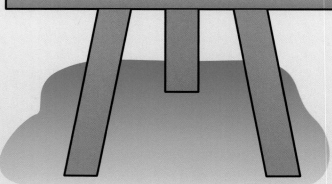

Homebound Bear

This homebound bear partners parents and children for phonemic awareness fun.

1. Nestle a teddy bear in an overnight bag. Also include a note explaining that the child and bear are to find up to five things from home that begin with the same sound as *bear*. Have the child place the items and bear in the bag and return the bag to school the next day.
2. During circle time, ask the child and bear to show their phonemic finds.
3. Invite a different child to take the bag and bear home to complete the same exercise.
4. Extend this activity throughout the school year by challenging youngsters to find items beginning with different sounds.

My Name Begins Like...

What's in a name? Plenty of beginning sound fun!

1. Program a sheet of paper with "My name begins like…" Make a class supply.
2. Give each child a copy along with an old magazine, scissors, and glue.
3. Have her cut out magazine pictures whose names begin the same way as her name. Direct her to glue them to the page.
4. Display the completed pages. Invite each child to choose a page, name the pictures and beginning sounds, and then identify the owner.

Guess My Word

Encourage thinking while reviewing beginning sounds with this quick guessing game.

1. Invite a child to think of an object.
2. Have him give the class several clues, one of which must be the sound the word starts with. For example, he may say, "I'm thinking of a word that starts like /m/. It's something you drink. It comes from a cow."
3. The first child to guess correctly thinks of the next object and gives clues.
4. Play several rounds, encouraging students to choose different sounds each time.

This is a carrot. Carrot starts with /k/.

It's in the Bag

Here's a simple circle-time activity that will reinforce beginning sounds.

1. Fill a paper grocery bag with empty plastic containers, empty cereal boxes, and plastic foods from your dramatic-play center.
2. Invite youngsters to pass the bag around the circle while reciting the rhyme below.
3. At the end of the rhyme, the child holding the bag will take out an item and then say its beginning sound (or blend). Encourage the rest of the class to repeat the initial sound.
4. Have students repeat the activity until the bag is empty.

Grocery shopping sure is fine;
Fill your cart and get in line.
Pay your bill and load your sack.
Then, next week, you'll be right back!

Ahh, an Alligator

Here's a snappy way to help youngsters identify items that begin with the same sound!

1. To decorate a shoebox to resemble an alligator, trim the lid to form teeth as shown; then paint the box white and green. Glue a paper eye to each of two polystyrene ball halves. Glue the ball halves to the top of the box along with two green pom-poms for the nose.
2. Fill the box with small items whose names all begin with the same sound.
3. Have a child reach inside the alligator's mouth and grab an item. Invite him to name the item and identify its beginning sound.
4. Play several rounds, guiding students to understand that the items' names all share the same beginning sound.

Letter-Sound Associations

This section consists of ideas that provide practice with:

- **naming letters and the corresponding sounds**
- **identifying the beginning letters of words**
- **recognizing words that begin with the same letter**

Shopping Sounds

A few paper grocery bags and clean, empty food containers can provide plenty of tasty letter-sound recognition practice!

1. Label each of three paper grocery bags with a different consonant. Making sure that each food name begins with one of the chosen consonants, set out empty plastic food containers, empty food boxes, and plastic foods from your dramatic-play center.
2. Invite youngsters to take turns sorting the foods into the correct bags.
3. When the foods are all sorted, empty one bag at a time and have students chorally name each item to confirm its placement. If a food does not belong in the bag, have a child place it in the correct bag.
4. Repeat the activity at another time with different consonants.

Catalog Sale

Shop for letter-sound awareness while giving old catalogs new life.

1. Explain to students that you're having a hard time shopping for gifts and need their help. Give each child an old catalog.
2. Write a consonant on the board, such as *M.* Say the name of the letter and its sound. Tell students they can buy anything in their catalogs that begins with that letter.
3. Have each child search his catalog for items that begin with the featured letter.
4. After a few minutes, invite students to name their items. Record the items on a chart. Have students visually confirm that each item's name begins with the featured letter and sound.

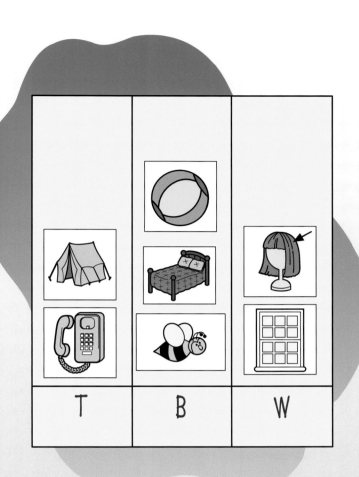

Letter Graphs

Here's a game that incorporates letter awareness with math.

1. On a length of bulletin board paper, prepare a three-column graph. Label each column with a different consonant.
2. Collect a quantity of small pictures of items whose names begin with the chosen consonants. (If desired, use selected picture cards from pages 220-224.) Write the corresponding name on the back of each picture. Store the pictures in a paper lunch bag.
3. Have each child, in turn, draw a picture from the bag, name the beginning letter and its sound, and then turn it over to check her answer. Have her tape her picture in the correct column.
4. When everyone has had a turn, discuss the graph results and name each picture to reinforce the letters and sounds.

Letters in the Mail

Little ones love to get mail, so send them some letters—the alphabet kind!

1. Place a real mailbox in your classroom. Each week, place a die-cut version of the letter you'll be studying inside the mailbox for youngsters to discover.
2. The next day, add a package with a letter-related surprise, such as apples for the letter *A* or bows for the letter *B*. Have students decide whether the package and letter match.
3. Add two or more surprise packages during the week and encourage youngsters to check the mail during circle time.

Letter Matchups

These simple puzzles are perfect for center use!

1. Lay two jumbo craft sticks side by side. With a marker, write a large letter as shown.
2. Draw a simple picture of an item whose name begins with that letter on the sticks in the same fashion.
3. Repeat Steps 1 and 2 to make several puzzles.
4. Store the puzzles in a center. Invite a child to spread the sticks on a table and then match each pair. As he works, encourage him to say each letter and name each object.

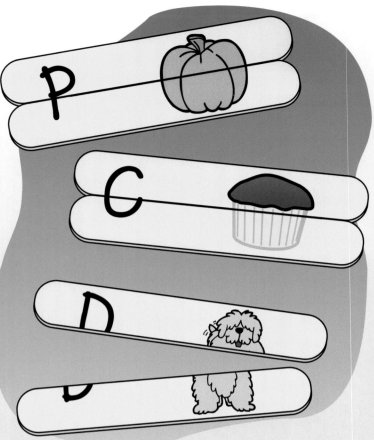

Letter Gardens

Here's a game that will sow some letter awareness.

1. During circle time, teach youngsters the rhyme below.
2. Tell students that the farmer planted only things whose names begin with those letters. Ask students to name things the farmer may have planted in the *T* row. Encourage each child to emphasize the *T* sound in her suggestion.
3. After naming a few *T* objects, move on to *P* and *D,* respectively.
4. At another circle time, change the letters and repeat the activity in this same manner.

Farmer, farmer, I'd like to know—
In your garden what does grow?
I see *T*s and *P*s and *D*s
All standing in even rows.

Weekly Snacks

Snacking on letter sounds is a fun way to remember them!

1. Ask your students to help you plan snacks for the week. Explain that you want to snack on foods whose names begin with the week's featured letter.
2. Record suggestions on the board, making sure to identify the beginning letter and its sound for each choice.
3. Consider pairing food choices for taste and availability, such as honey on crackers when focusing on *H.*
4. Serve a special letter snack each day of the week. Encourage students to name the snack and its beginning sound before eating.

Letter Putt

Score a phonemic hole in one with a center that combines letter-sound association with golfing!

1. Obtain a child's plastic golf set, or round up plastic golf balls, clubs, and cups.
2. Program each plastic golf ball with a letter your class has studied. Set up several holes in a center area. (If you're using plastic cups for holes, be sure to securely tape them to the floor.) Arrange an assortment of objects whose names begin with the programmed letters.
3. Have a child in this center try to putt a ball into a hole. When she sinks one, have her read the letter and then match the ball to one of the objects.
4. Have the child continue in this manner until all the balls and objects are matched.

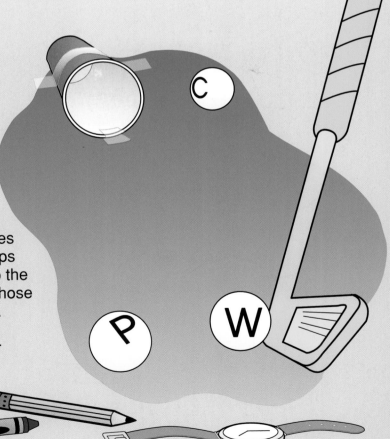

Flannelboard Matchup

Fuzzy, inviting felt is just the thing to help develop letter awareness!

1. Place several felt letters near the bottom of a flannelboard. Also place on the board a felt-backed picture of an item whose name begins with one of the featured letters.
2. Choose a volunteer to match the picture with its beginning letter.
3. Continue with other pictures and volunteers.

Letter Bracelets

Jewelry that's both stylish and functional? Sounds like a fabulous fashion statement!

1. Stock a center with 1" x 6" paper strips and crayons or markers.
2. Invite a child in this center to write a letter of her choice on her strip and then decorate the strip.
3. Help her use tape to fasten the completed bracelet around her wrist.
4. Throughout the day, encourage each student to read the room to find items whose names begin with her letter.
5. During an afternoon circle time, invite each child to take a turn naming her special letter and an item whose name begins with that letter.

Variation: When studying a specific letter, have each child make a bracelet featuring that letter. Then have students find items whose names begin with the letter.

Alphabet Big Books

This cooperative bookmaking experience will really spark your youngsters' interest!

1. Set up an alphabet center in your classroom. Each day, place a large sheet of construction paper or tagboard in the center. Write a large letter in the center of the sheet.
2. Stock the center with old magazines, scissors, glue, and stickers. Have each child, in turn, visit this center, read the day's letter, and then find a magazine picture or sticker of an item whose name begins with that letter. Have him attach the picture to the sheet.
3. When a sheet for each letter has been completed, bind the pages into a class book. Read the book together; then place it in your class library for continued enjoyment.

Letter Occupations

This student-made alphabet book takes a little extra time for students to make, but it's worth it!

1. In advance, place 26 sheets of paper in a binder. (You may wish to use hole reinforcers for durability.) Label each page with a letter from *A* to *Z.* Place the binder with old magazines and scissors in a center.
2. Invite a child in this center to look through the magazines for pictures of occupations that begin with the letters of the alphabet. For instance, she might find an astronaut for *A,* a baker for *B,* a conductor for *C,* or a dancer for *D.* When she finds a picture, she cuts it out and places it on the corresponding page in the binder.
3. During a circle time, go through the binder with students and review the picture choices. Invite children to name each occupation and its beginning letter. Then glue the picture onto the corresponding page. With students, brainstorm occupations for any pages without pictures. You may also wish to invite students to draw pictures for harder-to-find letters and occupations.

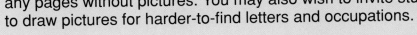

Sound Lotto

This twist on the time-honored favorite game is just right for your letter learners!

1. Make a class set of lotto boards by visually dividing large index cards into nine squares each. Program each square with a different letter. (Be sure to mix up the letters on each card.) Place a set of alphabet letter cards in a bag.
2. Give each child a gameboard and a supply of small paper squares to use as markers.
3. Draw a letter from the bag and say its sound. Have each child look on her gameboard for the letter that matches the sound. If she has it, direct her to cover it with a paper square.
4. Continue play until a child has three squares in a row covered and calls, "Sound Lotto!"

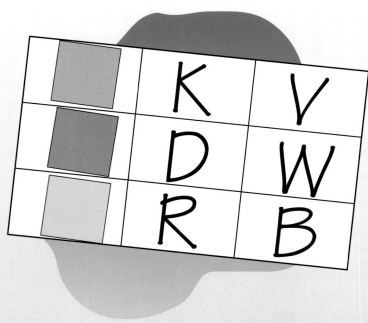

Beginning-Sound Sort

Practice sorting and beginning-sound identification with this game.

1. Choose three categories (such as clothing, animals, and toys) and three beginning sounds (such as /m/, /b/, and /d/). On each of three cards, draw an item in each category that begins with the first sound and write the item's name, underlining the beginning sound. Repeat for each sound so that you have a set of nine cards.
2. Lay the cards faceup on a table.
3. Ask a child to sort the cards by category.
4. Mix up the cards and ask another child to sort them by beginning sound. For additional practice, invite the child to name the pictured items and say their beginning sounds aloud.

Toy Box

Change this activity as often as desired to emphasize a different letter and sound.

1. Label a large cardboard box with a die-cut letter.
2. Encourage students throughout the day to fill the box with toys whose names begin with that letter's sound.
3. During a circle time, remove the toys one by one and review their names and beginning sounds. Have students put misplaced toys back into their proper spots.
4. Emphasize the letter sound by lining up the toys and then chorally naming them.

Same and Different

Which toys belong together? This game is sure to challenge youngsters!

1. Choose an assortment of toys whose names begin with the same sound. Place three on a table with one toy whose name begins with a different sound.
2. Invite students to name the toys and tell you which share the same beginning sound. Then have them name the toy that is different.
3. Ask a student to name the letter associated with the sound of the matching toys. Write the letter on the board.
4. Play again with a new set of toys and sounds.

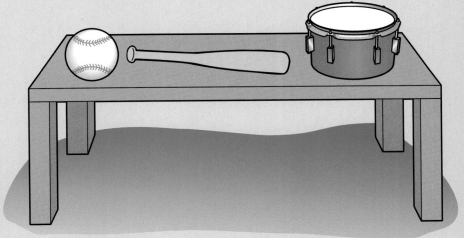

Animal Sounds

The correlation between an animal's name and the sound it makes is the perfect analogy for helping your students understand that a letter also has a name and a sound.

1. Name one animal at a time; then have students respond with the animal's sound.
2. Reverse the pattern and make one animal sound at a time, and ask students to respond with the animal's name.
3. Transition to letters by naming a letter and its sound and having students repeat.
4. Then name a letter and have students supply the sound.
5. Finally, say a letter sound and have students give the letter name.

A bear says ...

"Gr-r-r!"

Mystery Letter

Students will eagerly take turns to guess a mystery letter!

1. Choose a child to stand in front of the class.
2. Without showing it to him, tape a letter card to his back.
3. Have him call on student volunteers to say words beginning with his letter.
4. Have him use the word clues to guess the letter.
5. After he correctly guesses the letter, invite him to choose the next player to wear a letter card.

Henry can hop.

Name Actions

Kids can't help but get in on the action when you try this lively activity!

1. Give each child a name card, and gather students for a group-time activity.
2. Select one child to stand in front of the group, holding his name card.
3. Say the child's name twice and point out the first letter or sound in his name.
4. Say an action that starts with the same sound as the beginning sound in the child's name. For example, say, "Matt can march."
5. Have the child perform the action you named.
6. Continue with other students' names.

Food Sounds

Food, or at least the mention of it, adds interest to this activity.

1. In advance, label a small paper plate for each child with the beginning letter of the child's first name. Also draw a simple picture of a food whose name begins with the same beginning letter and sound. If desired, clippings from a magazine or stickers could be substituted for the drawing.
2. Give each child her plate.
3. In turn, ask each child to show her plate to the class. Lead the students in saying, "[Child's name] loves to eat [pictured food]." Then ask the child to tell everyone whether or not it is a true statement.

Sound Show-and-Tell

This version of show-and-tell is special because it involves each child's name as well as beginning letter sounds.

1. In advance, help each child identify the beginning sound in her name.
2. Ask each child to bring an item for show-and-tell whose name has the same beginning sound as her name.
3. During the designated sharing time, ask a child to stand. Say the child's name; then have the class name her object. Lead your students to recognize that the beginning sounds are the same.
4. Allow the student to share additional information about her item before having another child share.

bed

cake

pan

Picture Sounds

Old magazines are put to practical use when you make these handy picture cards.

1. Select some magazine pictures in which the objects' names represent letters and beginning sounds your class is studying.
2. Cut out and glue each picture to a separate large index card.
3. Label each card with the name of the object.
4. Select a card and show it to your class.
5. Discuss the object and name it, pointing out the beginning letter.
6. Ask if anyone in your group has a name that begins the same way. If so, have the students say the object name and the student's name aloud.

Turtle

Letter Stories

Your students will ask for this letter-inspired story activity again and again—and the outcome is never the same twice!

1. Place four to eight magnetic letters in a bag.
2. Begin to tell an impromptu story. Stop after a few sentences and have a student select a letter from the bag.
3. Have the child name the letter and say its sound; then have her name a word that begins with that sound.
4. Incorporate her word into the story as you continue.
5. Continue in this manner until the letters have all been chosen.

Letter Snacks

Turn snacktime into learning time with this tip.

1. For each day, plan for a snack whose name begins with a different letter of the alphabet.
2. Schedule the snack to match the letter you're studying on that day.
3. Before serving each snack, write its name on the board and point out the beginning letter. Have each child say the snack's name and the beginning sound before the snacking begins.

apple

I'm going to tell you a T story.

Story Starters

You won't have to ask twice for volunteers when you offer children opportunities to spin short tales using words that share initial consonants.

1. Write a different letter on each of six different index cards.
2. On each card, glue three or four pictures of words that begin with the letter indicated.
3. Store the cards in a bag or envelope.
4. At circle time, have a volunteer draw one of these cards without looking and then tell his classmates what letter is featured.
5. Have him tell a brief story that includes all the picture words on his card. The story could be just five or six sentences long.
6. Afterward, ask his classmates to recall some of the words the storyteller used that begin with the featured letter.
7. Have another child draw a card and repeat the process.

Animal Puppet Rhymes

Grins and giggles are a sure thing when you put puppets to work facilitating letter-sound associations.

1. Locate a type of puppet that begins with a letter your children have recently been discussing. For example, you might choose a moose puppet for *M*.
2. To begin this activity, write the kind of puppet on the board and underline the initial letter. Explain what initial sound and letter the puppet stands for.
3. Have the children suggest one other word that begins with the same sound and letter as the puppet. Write it on the board and underline the initial letter.
4. Have the puppet lead the children in the provided verse and insert the word the children suggested in the last line.
5. Repeat Steps 3 and 4 as many times as you'd like with the same puppet, inserting a different last word each time.
6. At another time, repeat Steps 1 through 5 using a different puppet, and adjust the wording of the verse accordingly.

moose
mustard

This little [moose] makes [m] words.
This little [moose] says [/m/].
This little [moose] says [m] words.
This little [moose] says, "[mustard]."

Monthly Letter-Sound Albums

Every time you turn another page on the calendar you have fresh inspiration for beginning-sound reinforcement.

1. Obtain a notebook with a clear plastic sleeve on the front.
2. For the cover, insert a child's seasonal artwork labeled with the current month and its beginning letter, such as "*J* Is for January."
3. Ask each child to think of something that relates to the current month for the subject of her page in the book.
4. On hole-punched paper, have her draw a picture or glue on one from a magazine. Support her as much as needed as she writes (or dictates for you to write) "[Letter] Is for [Object]."
5. Solicit children's help in getting the pages in alphabetical order and putting the pages in the notebook.
6. Place the book in your reading area and encourage children to read it to each other.

Rhyme Families

Children who have many of the earlier literacy skills well in hand will enjoy this once-a-week word-family activity.

1. Introduce your children to the -*at* family.
2. Start by writing "-at" on the board.
3. Write the name of one family member, Mat, on the board twice. Direct children's attention to one of the words. Discuss the -*at* in *Mat* and then blend the initial sound /m/ with -*at* to say the word *Mat*.
4. Erase the *M* from the name and ask your children to tell you what other letter could be used to make the name of a second family member. Write that letter where the *M* was. Blend the initial consonant with the -*at* ending as before and talk about the name that is made.
5. Write this name elsewhere on the board before erasing the initial consonant in the original name yet again.
6. Repeat Steps 3 and 4 as many times as desired. Then read all the rhyming family names that have been created.
7. Repeat the activity each week, using different word families, such as -*im*, -*on*, and -*en*.

Picture Cards A–E

Use with selected ideas as desired.

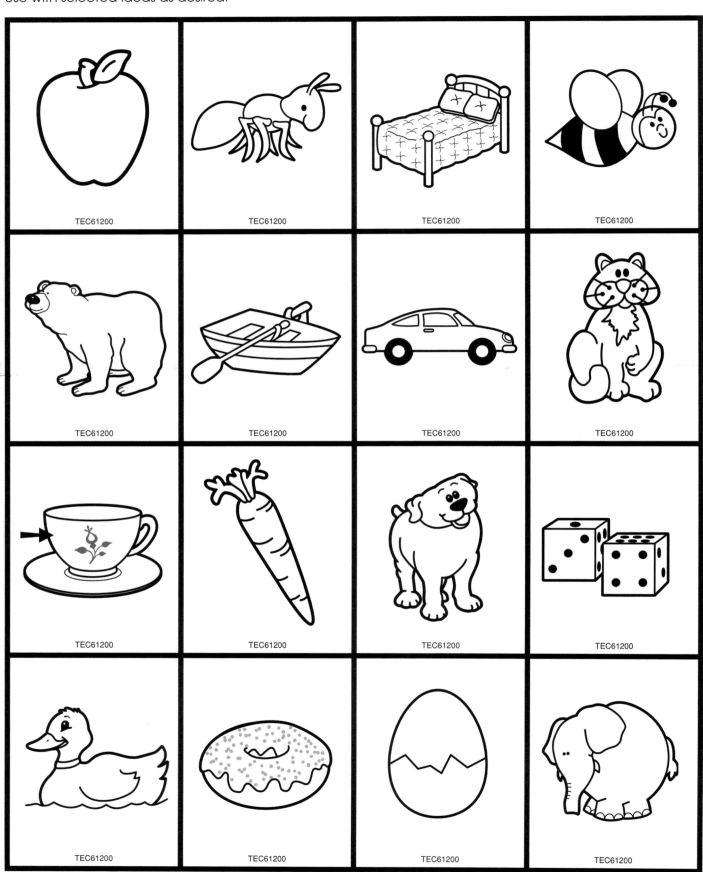

Picture Cards K–O

Use with selected ideas as desired.

TEC61200

TEC61200

TEC61200

TEC61200

TEC61200

TEC61200

TEC61200

TEC61200

TEC61200

TEC61200

TEC61200

TEC61200

TEC61200

TEC61200

TEC61200

TEC61200

222

TEC61200

TEC61200

TEC61200

TEC61200

TEC61200

TEC61200

TEC61200

TEC61200

TEC61200

TEC61200

TEC61200

TEC61200

TEC61200

TEC61200

TEC61200

TEC61200

Picture Cards T–Z

Use with selected ideas as desired.

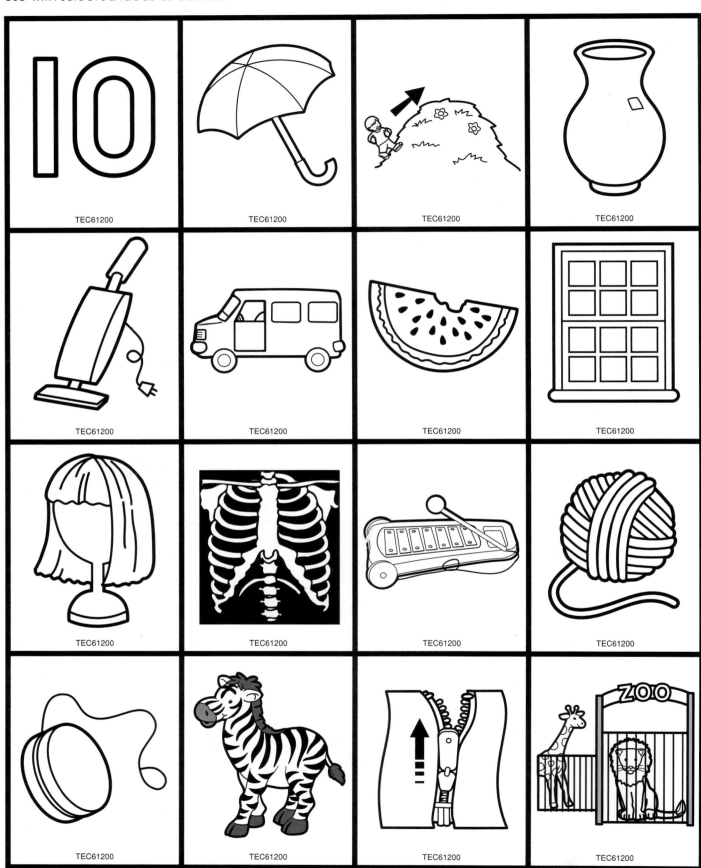

TEC61200	TEC61200	TEC61200	TEC61200
TEC61200	TEC61200	TEC61200	TEC61200
TEC61200	TEC61200	TEC61200	TEC61200
TEC61200	TEC61200	TEC61200	TEC61200